PRAISE FOR HARPER WELLS

Hilarious, heartfelt, and outrageously practical—this is the survival guide every woman over 60 deserves to have on her coffee table and in her back pocket.

> ROXIE DELGADO, 69, RETIRED NURSE AND LIFELONG GROUP-TEXT CONNOISSEUR

Finally, a survival manual that treats aging as a bold adventure, not a quiet retreat—funny, honest, and surprisingly wise.

> MIRA CALDERON, 64, FOUNDER OF THE SILVER LAUGHTER CLUB

Smart, sassy, and relentlessly kind, this book turns the chaos of growing older into a comedy you can actually use.

JUNE HOLLOWAY, 72,
COMMUNITY ORGANIZER AND
STORYTELLER

HILARIOUS SURVIVAL GUIDE FOR WOMEN OVER 60

HILARIOUS SURVIVAL GUIDE FOR WOMEN OVER 60

LAUGHS, LIFE HACKS, AND LIVING YOUR BEST LIFE AFTER 60

THE WOMEN'S SURVIVAL SERIES
BOOK 1

HARPER WELLS

Copyright © 2026 by Harper Wells

Published by Book Bound Studios

All rights reserved.

No part of this publication may be reproduced, distributed, or transmitted in any form or by any means, including photocopying, recording, or other electronic or mechanical methods, without the prior written permission of the publisher, except in the case of brief quotations embodied in critical reviews and certain other noncommercial uses permitted by copyright law.

Disclaimer: The information provided in this book is for educational and entertainment purposes only. The author and publisher make no representation or warranties with respect to the accuracy, applicability, fitness, or completeness of the contents of this book. The information contained in this book is strictly for educational purposes. Therefore, if you wish to apply ideas contained in this book, you are taking full responsibility for your actions.

The author and publisher disclaim any warranties (express or implied), merchantability, or fitness for any particular purpose. The author and publisher shall in no event be held liable to any party for any direct, indirect, punitive, special, incidental, or other consequential damages arising directly or indirectly from any use of this material, which is provided "as is," and without warranties.

First Edition

To the women who prove every day that sixty is not a curtain but a bright new stage—may your humor stay sharp, your courage unwavering, and your hearts open to joy. To my mother, sisters, friends, and all readers who choose laughter as a survival tool: this book is for you.

I am not afraid of storms, for I am learning how to sail my ship.

LOUISA MAY ALCOTT, LITTLE WOMEN (1868)

CONTENTS

Welcome to the Age of Not Caring (Mostly) — xiii

1. The Body's New Sound Effects and Other Plot Twists — 1
2. The Great Glasses Mystery (and Other Things You Lose Daily) — 19
3. Doctor Appointments, Tests, and the Art of Being Taken Seriously — 37
4. Menopause's Lingering Cameos (and Other Hormonal After-Parties) — 59
5. Retirement Reinvention—Now What Do I Do All Day? — 75
6. Friendship After 60—Your Circle, Your Rules — 91
7. Family Dynamics, Grandkids, and the Boundary Olympics — 109
8. Dating, Companionship, and "Do I Even Want This?" — 129
9. Tech, Social Media, and Scams—A Field Guide for the Brave — 149

10. Money, Downsizing, and the Stuff That Somehow Multiplied — 167

11. Confidence, Style, and Living Loudly (Even If Your Knees Object) — 185

The Sweet Freedom of This Season—Keep Laughing, Keep Choosing You — 205

WELCOME TO THE AGE OF NOT CARING (MOSTLY)

HOOKED BY A NEW SOUNDTRACK

On a Tuesday morning, you bend to pour a cup of tea and realize your knees have started their own podcast without your consent. The room fills with a chorus of pops, creaks, and a sly little wheeze that sounds suspiciously like a studio audience in your hips. The surprise isn't the noises themselves; it's that you can hear them and still smile. This is life upgrading itself, not a signal to retreat. Welcome to the soundscape you never asked for but you're now living in—a symphony of aging that feels intimate, ridiculous, and absolutely you.

If you're reading this, you're not asking for permission to laugh through the changes. You've got eyes that still spark with mischief, a calendar filled with plans, and a whole landscape of years behind you and ahead of you. You're part of a club that doesn't advertise membership, but once you're in, you're in for good: the over-60 crew that refuses to fade into a quiet corner when the lights come on. This book is your invitation to stay front and center, to treat aging as a stage you get to own, not as a curtain you're hauling around behind you.

Humor is not denial; it's a sturdy tool for navigating the quirks, the surprises, and the occasional indignities of later life. It offers clarity when the world throws five new terms at you in a single doctor's visit, and it turns the most ordinary days into stories you'll want to tell again and again. This book isn't about pretending you've become invincible or perfected your body into a museum piece. It's about acknowledging the new plot twists—the muffled hum of a coffee mug in the morning, the phone that seems to know exactly when you need a reminder, the energy that arrives in waves and sometimes takes a nap in between—and choosing to respond with courage, wit, and a dash of swagger.

So lean in. We'll talk about reading glasses with moods, group texts that require diplomatic skills, and the art of surviving the small silent wars with family, doctors, and your own schedule. We'll celebrate the freedoms this season grants—time to design your days, the stubborn wisdom that comes from years of practice, and the audacity to demand joy even when your body is busy negotiating with gravity. If you've ever wondered what it would feel like to age with a little more mischief and a lot more intention, you're in the right place. This isn't a pep talk masquerading as advice; it's a love letter to living on your own terms, with your own hair color, your own opinions, and your own unshakable sense of humor.

WHY THIS BOOK EXISTS (AND WHY NOW)

This book grew from a chorus of conversations that happen at kitchen tables, in library book groups, and in online communities where women 60 and older swap stories, tips, and a few well-telt exaggerations for good measure. We're living longer than ever, and the question isn't how to endure this season, but how to inhabit it with clarity, heat, and dignity. The market often sells youth as the currency of relevance; this book argues that the true wealth in your 60s and beyond is experience, boundaries, and the freedom to choose what matters and what doesn't. Aging is not a concession; it's a platform.

Humor is how we keep from shrinking when the world keeps asking us to. It's not frivolous, and it's certainly not evasive. It's a way to illuminate truth without burning bridges, to acknowledge limits while expanding what's possible. This book is not a sterile manual or a motivational slogan; it's a companion that speaks plainly, treats you like a grown person with a sparkling sense of humor, and gives you practical tools that actually fit real lives. You'll find pep talks that feel like a chat with a friend over coffee, and shamelessly honest truths about boundaries, menopause cameos, and retirement reinvention.

The aim is simple: help you navigate the

"new normal" with confidence and playfulness. You don't need to have everything figured out to begin; you just need to be willing to try a small, doable shift here and there. This book respects your autonomy, acknowledges the complexity of your days, and offers a gentle, sometimes goofy, stream of guidance that doesn't pretend aging is a flawless journey. It is, instead, a bold, often funny journey that you steer—one clever habit at a time.

Ultimately, this book is for the women who want to keep showing up—present, engaged, and loud enough to be heard in a room that's listening hard for silence. If you're newly retired, if you're living your best life at 70, if you're navigating the maze of technology and memories and family, or if you're simply seeking a brighter lens on a season that's been given a chance to shine, you've found your companion. The opportunity here isn't to pretend you're younger; it's to insist that you remain unmistakably, unapologetically you—and to do it with laughter.

WHAT YOU'LL FIND BETWEEN THESE PAGES

From the moment you open this book, you'll hear a familiar voice: warm, a touch cheeky, and never insulting. The pages invite you to stay awhile, to laugh, and to try small, practical steps that honor your life as it is today. You'll meet a cast of themes that echo the moments most of us face in this season: the body's new sound effects and plot twists; the Great Glasses Mystery that loves to vanish when you need them most; the delicate art of being taken seriously at doctor appointments without losing your sense of humor; menopause's lingering cameos that don't fade with time; and the ongoing project of retirement reinvention—rethinking purpose, day by day, on your own terms.

You'll also encounter the daily realities of friendship, family, and the tricky dance of boundaries. There's a steady thread about staying independent while leaning on practical support when needed, about embracing new technologies without becoming their hostage, and about recognizing that companionship—whether romantic, platonic, or fa-

WELCOME TO THE AGE OF NOT CARIN... xix

milial—can evolve into something richer with time, not thinner with fear. And yes, there are playful pep talks and frankly honest truths sprinkled throughout, because life after 60 doesn't require you to pretend you have everything under control, only that you keep moving forward with grace and humor.

Each chapter is designed as a friendly conversation rather than a rigid program. You'll meet Chapter 1's body at play, Chapter 2's keys and glasses going on "vacation," Chapter 3's art of being heard in medical rooms, and every subsequent chapter that follows life's popular dance card—retirement reinvention, friendship realignments, family boundaries that actually stick, late-life dating, tech that's mysterious but conquerable, money stories that deserve honesty, and a finish line where confidence and style arrive together, unafraid to shout a little. This book isn't about fixing you; it's about helping you curate a life that fits you on your best days and your most trying ones alike.

What unfolds here are stories you'll recognize as your own or ones you're suddenly curious to claim. You'll see practical, doable suggestions that won't require you to sign away your stubbornness or your sense of humor. You'll learn to protect your time, to say no without apology, and to say yes to the things that spark joy, even if they look a little imperfect. And you'll be reminded, again and again, that aging is not losing ground—it's expanding the theater where your voice can roar, with humor as your microphone and grace as your spotlight.

YOUR NEXT MOVE: HOW TO READ AND PLAY ALONG

This book isn't a syllabus so much as a passport to a livelier chapter of your life. It invites you to make it your own, to annotate, underline, dog-ear pages, and read aloud to a friend who loves a good laugh as much as you do. Start with a chapter a week if you like, or dip in for a few pages between a doctor's appointment and a grocery run. The pace is yours; the joy is the constant. A simple ritual—the pen, the page, and a cup of tea—can turn a casual read into a quiet, powerful practice of choosing joy in small, repeatable ways.

Seek out companions in your daily life: a friend who'll read alongside you, a book club where humor is as welcome as insight, or a family member who will listen to your reflections without offering unsolicited advice. This book thrives on conversation, so feel free to discuss what you've learned, what made you laugh hardest, and which tips you're most likely to try in the coming week. The more you engage with the ideas here, the more they'll start to feel like second nature, woven into your ordinary rhythms rather than tacked on as extra work.

Remember: the goal isn't to become flawless or pretend you don't notice the changes. It's to honor your years with a voice that's both clear and kind, a wardrobe that fits you now, and a daily life that feels like you—bold, practical, and wonderfully funny. This book is your invitation to rewrite the narrative of aging as a dynamic, generous, and very human adventure. So turn the page with curiosity, trust your own judgment, and let the next chapter begin with a laugh that opens doors you didn't know existed.

ONE

THE BODY'S NEW SOUND EFFECTS AND OTHER PLOT TWISTS

THE SYMPHONY OF SNAPS, CRACKS, AND SURPRISE NOISES

If you walk into a room and your knees announce your entrance before you do, you're not imagining things. Your body has its own little symphony now, a quirky, sometimes melodious, sometimes alarming soundtrack that follows you around like an obliging, occasionally stubborn chorus. The first time you hear your hip crack in the grocery store, you glance around to see if anyone noticed. Spoiler alert: they did not notice the crack, but they did notice you flinch. Aging isn't a cinematic fade to black; it's a continuous, often comic, soundtrack with new voices and unfamiliar instruments. And yes, a lot of it is perfectly normal. Your joints aren't misbehaving so much as they're auditioning for a starring role in the life you're still learning how to direct.

What matters is not whether your body sounds like a drumline at a parade, but how you respond when the music swells. This is your cue to befriend the quirks rather than pretend they don't exist. Start with a simple daily routine that respects the tempo of your new tempo: a few minutes of easy movement to wake things up, some light stretches that loosen the stiffness without scaring your joints, and a moment of appreciation for the fact that you can still move at all. No dramatic overhauls are required; think of it as a friendly upgrade rather than a renovation project that erases the old you.

Consider the practical side of this new soundtrack. Supportive footwear with a gentle tread can make a surprising difference; a chair with proper height and back support can save your spine from post-lunch drama, and a standing desk setup can reduce the cello-like sighs your knees emit after a long day of sitting. Hydration turns out to be a secret agent. Water lubrication is a thing—your joints thank you when you give them a steady drizzle of hydration rather than a parade of dehydrated afternoons. Calibrating your movements to be kinder to aging joints doesn't mean giving up things you love; it means preserving them longer, with more laughter and fewer creaks as you go.

Tips and rituals that work in concert with the body's new soundtrack are not about denial; they're about negotiation. If a morning stretch loosened the morning-person in you, you've already won half the battle. If a midafternoon stroll lightens the mood and lightens the ache, you've struck a sweet balance. You'll notice that most big changes here are small, forgiving, and repeatable. A minute spent warming up before you step into the day can keep your ankles from sounding like castanets at a conductor's rehearsal. A five-minute cooldown after any activity—lifting groceries, gardening, or a quick dance in the kitchen—helps the body remember what it was doing and keeps the chorus from wandering into discord.

In the end, this chapter invites you to give your body a standing ovation for the performance it's still delivering. You may be dealing with new noises, but you're also reclaiming agency over them. You can choose the tempo, you can choose the instruments you want to hear, and you can choose to laugh when the trumpet of an elbow squeak concerts in the middle of a quiet room. In short, you're not listening to your body's complaints so much as conducting a more harmonious score. And the first act is about normalizing the soundscape while laying down practical, achievable ways to ease the discomfort without turning life into a full-time medical regimen.

As you turn the page into the next scene, remember this: the body's new sound effects aren't a verdict on your vitality; they're a reminder of the stage you're still mastering. It's your show, and the audience—the family, the friends, the inner skeptic—will cheer you on when you make the music feel a little more like a lullaby and a little less like a courtroom drama.

ENERGY LEVELS: THE "WHY AM I TIRED?" EDITION

If fatigue had a personality, it would be that friend who nods at your plans and then schedules a nap in the middle of the coffee aisle. Energy isn't a fixed resource anymore; it's a currency you spend with intention, precision, and a touch of mischief. The truth most women over sixty learn the hard way is simple and oddly liberating: some days you'll feel like a spark, other days like a flicker, and both are perfectly acceptable. The goal isn't heroic endurance; it's practical wisdom about how to use the energy you have, when you have it, without slipping into guilt for needing rest.

The concept of "real" stamina after sixty isn't about pushing through to a heroic finish line. It's about aligning your daily map with the true landscape of your energy. You'll notice that certain hours feel brighter, warmer, or more focused. Others wear you down with the severity of a long winter. The trick is to plan around these rhythms rather than pretend they don't exist. In practice, this means scheduling demanding tasks for your peak energy windows and reserving lighter activities for the slower times. It also means recognizing that rest is not a failure but a strategic refresh—like charging your phone in the middle of the day so you stop scrambling when you most need power.

A few practical ways to steward energy without it turning into a full-time science project: start with a simple daily rhythm. Wake up with a routine that gently nudges you into motion rather than jolts you awake with a jolt. A light, protein-forward breakfast can steady the morning caffeine dash, which should be mindful rather than habitual. If you can fit in a 10-minute walk, it may do more to lift spirits and energy than an extra hour of scrolling. And yes, sometimes a nap is the right tool, not a sign of weakness. Short, targeted naps—20 minutes or so—can reset the mood and sharpen decision-making without leaving you groggy. The aim is to befriend fatigue rather than fight it with guilt and self-critique.

There will be days when energy feels scarce, and that's when a recalibration becomes essential. On those days, ask yourself a few simple questions: What tasks actually require energy right now, and what can wait?

How can I batch similar activities to minimize gear-switching—phone calls with a walking break, or emails after a short stretch? Can I move in smaller increments that fit around a favorite podcast or a beloved TV show? Small adjustments built into your day add up, and they don't demand a heroic endurance blowout. They demand consistency, a sense of humor, and the willingness to declare that rest is part of strategy, not a confession of weakness.

The section ends with a gentle reminder: your energy isn't a fixed number you're expected to guard like a priceless heirloom. It's a living, fluctuating asset that responds to care, routine, and kindness toward your own limits. As you shift toward a more intentional grid of activity, you'll notice not only fewer crashes but more moments you can fully enjoy—moments of ease in the middle of a busy week, a walk that doesn't ache, a task that feels almost doable rather than a mission impossible. And that, dear reader, is how you begin to turn fatigue from a mystery into a manageable companion who politely asks for a pause rather than a full surrender statement.

Get ready for the next scene, where sleep

enters the plot with its own brand of negotiation, slyly testing how well you've learned to advocate for rest.

SLEEP: THE NIGHTLY NEGOTIATION

Sleep is the daily contract you never signed but somehow agreed to when you said yes to living a full, loud, love-filled life. It's the one arena where reality often outsmarts intention, and still, it offers a clean slate every night. When you're in midlife, sleep isn't just about quantity; it's about quality, consistency, and finding a rhythm that your body can trust even when its clock seems to be running on a new, mysterious time zone. The good news is that sleep is a skill you can relearn with a few small, stubborn commitments and a sense of humor about the occasional late-night brain monologue about your to-do list.

Begin with the setup: a wind-down that's more ritual than routine, more curiosity than obedience. The room becomes a quiet stage where your nervous system lowers the lights and your thoughts learn to stand by. A cool, dark room sends a message to your body that it's time to retire the day's bravado. Darkness isn't punishment; it's signaling. If you can, dim the lights early, invest in blackout curtains, and keep the bedroom a device-free sanctuary. Screens, those glowing pressure points of modern life, deserve their own exit song: turn them off at least an hour before bed, or switch to a gentle mode that reduces blue light. If you must wander toward your phone in the night, keep the habit to a minimum and keep it out of reach so the snooze button becomes a safer option rather than a reflex.

Rituals matter more than brute force. A simple, repeatable pre-sleep sequence—warm bath or shower, soft music, a few minutes of slow, deliberate breathing—signals to your body that rest is the next destination. Hydration in the evening should be mindful, not heroic; a small sip when you wake helps you maintain balance, but a flood of liquid can lead to midnight alarms. The bed should be a sanctuary: comfortable mattress, supportive pillow, and a temperature that feels just-right cool rather than a room-temperature sauna. If you wake during the night, resist the urge to treat the clock as an adversary. Instead, focus on a calm reentry: return to breath, maybe a gentle stretch in bed or chair, and remind yourself that the body's built-in reset button is often a few minutes away.

There is also value in honoring the art of daytime naps. A short, crisp nap can be a blessing when offered gently and without judgment. A good rule is to keep naps brief, early in the afternoon, and linked to a specific need—refuel before a late afternoon appointment, or simply give your brain a gentle reset after a morning of heavy thinking. If you do not need a nap, a lighter alternative can be a quiet moment of rest, a period of meditation, or a slow walk outside. The objective is not to become nocturnal or to shrink your world but to restore balance so that sleep at night isn't a battle but a restoration.

The beauty of this nightly negotiation lies in its honesty. There will be nights when sleep resists your best-laid plans, and that's not a personal indictment. It's information you can use: adjust, experiment, and return to the practice. You are not failing; you're collecting data about your own rhythm and creating a reliable framework for tomorrow. As you begin to understand your cycles—your naturally fluctuating energy, your craving for quiet, your need for movement—you'll hear a whisper of quiet confidence: you can control the tempo of rest without surrendering the rest of your life. And with that confidence comes more mornings where you wake up feeling more at home in your own skin, more ready to greet the day with humor and purpose.

PAIN VS. "NEW NORMAL"

Pain changes the script without asking for permission. It can be a sharp intruder or a subtle undertone that hums in the background, a constant reminder that your body has changed its language and your job is to learn the new vocabulary without losing the sense of self that existed before. The line between a mere nuisance and a signal that something needs medical attention isn't always clear-cut. Too often we treat every ache as a crisis to be managed with the same intensity and fear we once reserved for bigger life moments. Your task is to become fluent in this new dialect: when to shrug, when to adapt, and when to seek a hand from a professional who can translate the pain into a plan.

The instinct to push through pain is powerful. It's a remnant of the past, a stubborn reminder that you're still the same person who climbed stairs with gusto and carried the world in a tote bag. But some signs deserve a different response: a persistent ache that lingers beyond a few days, a sudden sharp pain after a routine movement, swelling or deformity, or pain that wakes you at night. These are not things to dismiss; they're signals you've earned the right to listen to. This isn't about giving in to fear or letting the body dictate your identity. It's about respecting your boundaries and seeking guidance when the message of pain becomes louder than the message of your shared history with health and vitality.

Practical, everyday approaches can help before you reach for the medical pen. Gentle movement becomes a daily ally rather than a punishment: careful knee bends, ankle circles, or a slow walk can keep joints lubricated and muscles awake without pushing you over a line. Heat and cold therapies have their own quiet wisdom. A warm bath after a long day eases stiff joints; a cool compress on a localized ache can calm irritated tissue. A simple pain diary can turn scattered clues into a story you can share with a clinician: date, what you were doing, the intensity on a scale of 1 to 10, and the relief you felt after movement or rest. This isn't tattling on your body; it's producing an honest conversation you can bring to a visit with your doctor, physical therapist, or nurse practitioner.

There are times when the pain is a dependable companion, and there are times when it's a flare that asks for professional attention. The difference lies in how you respond: with curiosity, documentation, and a plan that respects both your independence and the legitimate need for care. The aim is not to erase pain but to coexist with it in a way that preserves your dignity, your mobility, and your ability to enjoy the little joys of everyday life—the same joys you've earned through decades of showing up with courage and humor.

The final note in this section is a reminder that a new normal isn't a surrender; it's the next version you. You can adapt, you can advocate, and you can still tell the stories that keep you warm at the table. There will be days with more questions than answers, and that's okay. The point is to approach pain with a clear voice and a steady compass, so you stay the author of your own health story while you keep laughing through the plot twists.

TINY HABITS THAT MAKE A BIG DIFFERENCE

Small changes don't demand a standing ovation; they ask for steady, repeated applause. Tiny habits are the unglamorous, dependable sidekicks that quietly transform the texture of your days: a few minutes of movement, a sip of water, a deliberate breath, a posture check, a moment of gratitude. The magic lies in repetition, not in fireworks. The aim is to build a few gentle routines that become so embedded in your day they're invisible but always there when you need them.

Let's start with something you can do in under five minutes, anywhere. A gentle morning movement that takes as little as 2–3 minutes can set the tone for hours: a handful of slow neck tilts, shoulder rolls, hip circles, and ankle rotations. This isn't about forcing yourself into a yoga pose you hate; it's about acknowledging the body's new language with tenderness and a touch of play. Do it while you wait for the kettle to boil or before you step into the shower, and you'll notice a surprising lift in mood and mobility without demanding a liftoff of your calendar.

Hydration is the most forgiving habit of all. A simple target—two glasses of water with the first coffee or tea of the day, and another couple by midmorning—can quiet the brain fog that mocks your focus. It's not a punishment for neglect; it's a cooperative routine that protects joints, supports digestion, and even helps skin feel a little more forgiving on the days when everyone is looking for the glow that older selfies insist you should have.

Communication becomes a tiny habit, too. A daily check-in with a friend, a family member, or a neighbor in the form of a short text or a quick call keeps your social energy robust and your boundaries clear. It's less about keeping score and more about maintaining the humans who root for you, while you learn to say "not tonight" to the things that drain you. Boundaries don't have to be dramatic; they can be the simplest, most honest version of yes and no that respects your time and your energy.

Movement and posture get their own little daily recital. A few minutes of posture-focused micro-work—gentle sits-to-stands, wall slides, or a slow doorframe stretch—can yield a surprising dividend in balance and calm. You don't need a gym membership to keep your body on your side; you need a mirror, a timer, and a willingness to do the focused, tiny work that compounds over weeks into real confidence and less pain.

Finally, a reminder: celebrate the wins, no matter how modest. The day you choose to pace yourself, the day you decide to nap without guilt, the day you stand up taller when you catch sight of a reflective surface—these are wins, not concessions. The cumulative effect of small, consistent choices is a soundtrack of progress that you can hear when you listen closely, and it's always worth the soft, stubborn cheer you give yourself for showing up.

As you close this chapter and step into the rest of the book, carry with you a few faithful allies: gentle mobility, steady hydration, clear boundaries, and a habit basket full of tiny, doable actions. They're not flashy, but they're reliable. They're the practical, warm-hearted tools you'll reach for again and again as you continue to write your life's story with humor, resilience, and a generous dose of your own remarkable spirit.

TWO
THE GREAT GLASSES MYSTERY (AND OTHER THINGS YOU LOSE DAILY)

THE READING GLASSES BERMUDA TRIANGLE

If there were a Bermuda Triangle for your sight, it would be hidden in the cushions of your couch, tucked behind the cereal box, and somehow orbiting the coffee table in that polite, infuriating way that says I was here—and so were these readers you can never seem to find when you need them most. You know the drill: you're mid-sentence, mid-chapter, mid-sip, and your glasses decide to ghost you. One moment they're perched on your head, the next they've vanished into that land beneath the sofa where missing coins go to retire. You swear they grew legs and marched off to book club without you, while you squint at the menu and pretend you can read the tiny print with the enthusiasm of a cat eyeing a sunbeam.

This is the Reading Glasses Bermuda Triangle: a triangular pocket universe where the objects you rely on for clarity disappear, reappear in the oddest places, and somehow always arrive with a headline about you misplacing them yet again. It's not a moral failing, dear reader. It's aging's way of teaching you a new superstition: always know where your glasses are before you start any sentence you intend to finish.

So how do we tame this chaos without turning every room into a surveillance zone for eyewear? You start with a system that respects both the humor of the situation and your sanity. First, we create glasses stations, intentionally placed like friendly outposts around your day. A sturdy tray by the entryway that holds a pair, a cleaning cloth, and a little note that says hello and stay. A second station by the bed so you don't wander in a daze into a world where reading the clock requires a magnifying glass and a magnifying glass requires an exponent. A third by the living room chair, because comfort and proximity tend to be the most persuasive arguments against accidental blindness.

Next comes the ritual: when you set eyes on a book, a menu, or a crossword, you pause for a micro-moment and ask, where did I last use these? If you can't answer in under five seconds, you pivot to the nearest glasses station and start the search with your eyes already trained on a predictable destination. If you find yourself tempted to blame gravity or a mischievous home appliance, you're not alone. Humor is your ally here. Every time you catch yourself hunting for your own glasses, take a breath, smile, and acknowledge that you and your glasses are in a long, ridiculous relationship that occasionally misplaces itself just to keep things interesting.

Color coding helps too. Pick a color for each station and stick with it. Red for the entryway, blue for the bed, green for the chair by the TV. Not only will it be easier to remember where to return them, it will also reduce the cognitive load when you're juggling a phone, a tote bag, and a tote full of grocery lists. And yes, invest in a spare pair—one in the car, one in the kitchen drawer, one in your purse—so you're never caught in the glow of a fluorescent hospital light while your sight slips away like a dramatic cliffhanger.

Remember this simple truth: you don't have to become a patron saint of organization to win this game. You just need to set up a few forgiving, reliable habits that resemble a routine rather than a jail sentence. The goal isn't perfection; it's a practical, repeatable pattern that buys you back a few minutes of not squinting at every sentence you read. And if a pair of readers still goes rogue, you'll at least have a story to tell at book club about the day the glasses started a preliminary vacation without you.

Now that your glasses have their own little outposts, you're primed to tackle the next big mystery: locating the phone that thinks it's playing hide-and-seek in your own hand. Stay tuned; what you learn next will make you wonder how you ever functioned without a memory that knows exactly where your phone is, even when it's pretending not to be there.

WHERE DID I PUT MY PHONE? (IT'S IN YOUR HAND)

If you think you've never misplaced something essential, think again. Your phone is not just a device; it's the most committed prankster in your life. It follows you around with the devotion of a loyal puppy, then hides in your hand or in the most inconvenient pocket, and acts as if it's been there all along while you frantically search the room for it. You'll hear the buzz, you'll feel the nudge, and you'll eventually realize the little rascal has been in the one place you refused to check: your own grasp. This is what we call the paradox of daily life in the age of smart technology: your pocket knows you better than you know it, and yet your brain decides to pretend that the device is a totally separate species that only reveals itself when it's too late.

The truth is, the phone is a master of misdirection. It hides in the obvious and reveals itself only after you've built a small shrine to it in your mind. You set it down to grab lipstick, it slides into your palm the moment you look away, and suddenly you're chasing a ghost that keeps pinging you from within. But fear not. We can outsmart this trickster with a simple, human-sized system that respects the dignity of your aging brain while honoring the phone as an essential partner in your daily mischief.

First, claim a designated pocket or pouch for the phone and keep it there. It doesn't have to be fancy; a small coach bag with a single phone-pocket suffices, as long as you use it consistently. If you're carrying a tote that weighs as much as a small suitcase, consider a detachable phone wallet that attaches to the strap. The goal is to reduce decision fatigue: when you reach for the device, you already know where to find it without launching a mental scavenger hunt.

Second, make a habit of a quick, two-step check before you move. Look at the surface you're standing on, then check your hand to confirm the phone is indeed in its appointed place. It sounds almost too simple, but the human brain loves simple rituals that don't require an engineering degree. The moment you step away, you'll instinctively feel that you should either quiet the ping or silence the siren worry that you've left it somewhere spectacular, like the fridge, or the laundry hamper, or the pocket of a jacket you wore once in 2014.

Third, give your phone a tiny, tactile cue. A bright strap, a chunky popsocket, or a neon bumper on the case can transform your relationship with the device from stealthy to obvious. You'll thank yourself when you're rushing through a store and your phone's silhouette announces itself with the confidence of a diva on opening night. And yes, take advantage of the tech you already own. Use the Find My feature, set up location alerts, and allow yourself the small thrill of hearing the device locate itself like a tiny, obedient beacon in the midst of your day.

If you find yourself in the middle of a sentence and your phone still eludes you, pause and perform one more check with humor as your guide. It's easy to slip into a spiral of self-reproach, but the real secret is kindness—toward yourself and toward the device that's doing its very best to keep pace with your fabulous life. The moment you've tamed the phone, you'll gain not just time but the reassurance that you're still in control of the clock, the calendar, and the next witty text from your group chat. And speaking of bags, our next stop is a different kind of internet-famous confusion: the purse that seems to contain everything except what you need most.

Next up, the Purse/Bag of Infinite Objects, where the mystery of the multiverse that lives inside your handbag meets the art of disciplined good taste.

THE PURSE/BAG OF INFINITE OBJECTS

If you've ever opened your handbag and felt the tug of gravity pulling every last object into a black hole of receipts, lipstick, and stray pens, you know the truth: your purse is not a bag. It's a living museum of your daily life, a portal that swallows attention and exerts mild, constant pressure to pull out every piece of evidence you've ever touched. It's the bag of infinite objects, a place where you can discover a shopping list you wrote in 2011, a receipt for a sweater that no longer fits, a packet of tissues that somehow multiplied, and a stray charger that you're certain belongs to a device you no longer own. The drama of the purse is less about chaos and more about identity—because every item tells a story about who you were when you last used it and who you are becoming now.

The first act in taming the purse is restraint that feels like kindness rather than punishment. Start with purpose: decide what you actually need to carry every day. If your daily reality doesn't require a full makeup kit or a dozen loyalty cards, reduce them to a lean set. This isn't a purge, it's a prioritization. Your core items might include a wallet with ID and essentials, a compact lipstick, a medicated item if necessary, tissues, a notepad and pen for those moment when you suddenly remember something you promised to do, and a compact phone or reading device that doesn't weigh you down. The aim is to shrink the bag's personality so it stops trying to be a portable version of your entire life.

With the essentials defined, the next move is organization that feels like a spa day for your belongings. Invest in small pouches or pouches that slide inside the bag like perfectly behaved guests. Color-coding helps—one color for receipts, another for meds, a third for tech items. The real magic is in the details: a tiny zipper pocket for change who might otherwise roll away into oblivion; a dedicated card slot to keep your most-used items easily accessible; a slim envelope by the front for those appointment reminders that arrive with alarming frequency. In other words, create zones inside the bag where your things can live with dignity, rather than participating in a chaotic scavenger hunt every time you reach for them.

We can go deeper with the ritual of maintenance. A weekly purse audit becomes a small, joyous ritual rather than a dreaded chore. Dump everything onto a flat surface, thank each item for its service, and ask whether you would choose it again today. If the answer is no, it goes into the donation box or into the recycling bin of good intentions. If it's a maybe, ask yourself what role it plays in your current life. If the role is no longer relevant, it's time to pass it along with a gentle smile.

The most important part of this process is memory: you want to remember that you have a purse with infinite objects, but you don't want the objects to remember you as the person who can't decide what to carry. So, keep a small daily checklist either in your phone or on a tiny card inside the purse. Before you leave the house, confirm you've got ID, keys, a form of payment, and your essential item of the week. It sounds small, but it creates a sense of steadiness that can ripple outward, affecting the way you move through the day with less friction and more confidence.

As you resume your day with fewer ghost items weighing you down, you're ready to face another kind of daily chaos: the act of decluttering with humor, patience, and boundaries. And if you're wondering how to handle the emotional side of letting go, the next section has you covered with a practical, compassionate approach to downsizing without a meltdown.

DECLUTTERING WITHOUT A MELTDOWN

Decluttering is less about erasing your past and more about carving out space for the life you want to live now. For many of us, the thought of downsizing or parting with keepsakes can feel personal, almost like a rejection of the memories tied to each item. But there's a kinder, more sustainable way to approach it: a process that respects your emotions while creating room for the things that actually support the life you're building today.

Start with small, manageable steps. Pick one drawer, one shelf, or one corner that no longer serves you and commit to a one-hour session. The clock becomes your ally rather than your enemy. You'll be surprised how much you can accomplish in sixty focused minutes when you're not trying to tackle the entire house at once. During that hour, you'll notice a familiar pattern: you keep items because of what they represented in a moment, not because they support your present self. It's not a betrayal to let go of a memory if it's released with gratitude and replaced by something that honors who you are now.

Boundaries deserve their own honorary place in this process. Boundaries with your own time, with family who wants to hold onto items that aren't yours to keep, and with the emotional weight of stuff that no longer fits your life. You'll have to say no to the well-intentioned, while still saying yes to the things that spark joy, or at least usefulness, in your daily routine. The trick is to reframe decluttering as an act of generosity toward yourself: you're giving yourself the gift of breathing room, of a home that serves you rather than a museum you must tour every day.

As you move through your belongings, bring humor along for the ride. Picture your items as characters in a long-running soap opera—the moral is not to forget where you came from, but to celebrate where you're headed. When you pause too long over a cherished object, ask yourself what it would take to keep the memory intact without keeping the object itself. A photograph, a quick written note, or a memory tucked into a journal can preserve the meaning without the physical weight. If you still feel a sting, invite a friend to join the process. A second pair of eyes can offer perspective and a dose of encouragement that makes the process feel less like a moral exam and more like a conversation among allies.

Downsizing is not a one-step sprint; it's a series of small, repeatable choices that build a life you're excited to live. It's about carving out time for the things you actually want to do and the people you want to be with, rather than the items you think you should keep because they belong to some version of you that no longer exists. And if the meltdown threatens to show up, remember to pause, breathe, and give yourself permission to step away until you can return with clarity and a little humor. After all, humor is the pantry where resilience is stored; it keeps you nourished as you navigate the emotional terrain of letting go.

When you've tidied the physical space, you'll find a surprising truth: the more you shed, the more you discover about your present priorities. You'll breathe easier, you'll sleep more soundly, and you'll notice that your days feel lighter, not because you've reduced your belongings to a minimalist's dream, but because you've aligned what you own with who you are today. That alignment is worth a thousand well-folded boxes. And as you close this chapter of clutter, you'll feel a steady invitation to the next: memory, distraction, and the art of living with intention in a world that never stops moving.

MEMORY VS. DISTRACTION

Is it memory or is it distraction? The truth is, both are part of the same modern experience, and the difference often matters less than the relief of having a system that works for you. Memory isn't a superpower you lose overnight; it's a practice you can strengthen with simple, repeatable rituals. Distraction, on the other hand, is a squirrel with a sparkly tail that runs across your path the moment you start a task. The trick isn't to pretend the distraction doesn't exist; it's to build structures that guide your attention back to what matters without turning your day into a scavenger hunt for misplaced cognitive energy.

A practical approach starts with external memory aids that stay you on track rather than begging your brain to remember every tiny detail. A simple notebook that remains open to today's tasks, a calendar where you write reminders in bold ink, and a few sticky notes placed in predictable, visible places can make a world of difference. The moment you write something down, you're effectively telling your brain, this is important; the memory doesn't have to carry the entire burden on its own. The combination of writing things down and keeping a consistent routine creates a predictable rhythm that your aging brain loves and your daily life rewards.

To distinguish between memory lapses and ordinary distraction, try a small test: when you forget something, ask yourself whether you paused to plan the action in advance or if you got sidetracked by something shiny and unrelated. If the answer leans toward planning, you've likely experienced a genuine memory moment. If it leans toward distraction, it's a reminder to adjust your environment, not your intelligence. The goal is not perfection but reliability: a few keystone habits you can lean on when your mind feels crowded and busy and your schedule grows heavy with obligations.

Tools help, but so does sleep, nutrition, and movement. A rested mind is less likely to skip a step because it's tired, and regular movement keeps your brain flexible and alert in ways that caffeine never can. Consider a daily ritual that combines light exercise with a cuppa to prime your brain for focus. It's not a magic wand, but it's a steady practice that reduces the chaos and increases the moments of clarity that matter.

As you adopt these memory-friendly habits, you'll begin to notice a subtle shift: you're less likely to react in panic when you realize you forgot something, because you have built-in systems that catch most things before they slip. You'll be more honest with yourself about what you can realistically remember and what you should record. And you'll discover that memory isn't a one-time achievement but a daily choice—a practice you cultivate in small, manageable chunks.

With these strategies in hand, you're ready to navigate a world that never slows down without losing your sense of humor or your sense of self. The path ahead—doctor appointments, dating, retirement reinventions—will still have its surprises, but you'll meet them with a toolkit that honors both your experience and your wit. And if a missing item or a missed deadline briefly tries to throw you off, remember the two truths you've learned here: you can make chaos manageable, and you can laugh about it while you do.

THREE
DOCTOR APPOINTMENTS, TESTS, AND THE ART OF BEING TAKEN SERIOUSLY

YOUR APPOINTMENT ARMOR

Speed dating with fluorescent lights and a clipboard—that's what a doctor visit often feels like, and somehow you're always left paying the cover charge for a mystery you didn't buy a ticket to. If you've ever walked out wondering what just happened and whether you remembered to ask for the important thing, you're not imagining things. The right prep turns this chaotic ritual into a collaboration, a moment where you're seen, heard, and in charge without needing a cape or a whistle. This is your appointment armor

—the mental, practical, and a little bit cheeky gear that helps you walk in with confidence and walk out with a plan.

Before you walk in, assemble your personal health dossier. Not a novel, just a clean, honest snapshot of where you've been and where you want to go. Bring your photo ID and your insurance card, always. Add a current medications list, including over-the-counter drugs and supplements, and note any allergies or adverse reactions you've had. Have a concise medical history ready, not a memoir, focusing on the conditions that matter now and the big ones that might influence future care—things like surgeries, chronic illnesses, and a quick note about family health red flags when relevant. If you've had recent lab results or imaging, tuck copies into a folder you can hand over or upload to the clinic's portal; the goal is to avoid chasing data halfway through the appointment.

Then create a short list of your concerns and goals for the visit. You don't need a three-page manifesto, but you do want to steer the conversation so you leave with clarity. Think of this like writing a tiny mission statement: What do you want to understand better? What options do you want to consider? What would a successful appointment look like for you—whether that's a clear plan, a specific test, or a follow-up call with a nurse who can translate the big words you're about to hear into plain English? If you have a trusted friend or family member who can join you, consider bringing them as a support person—their presence can help you stay on track and calm any nerves without turning the visit into a public trial.

Now, set an agenda in real time. Arrive early enough to complete forms and catch your breath, but not so early that you're bracing for your first fluorescent sunset of the day. When the exam room door opens, greet the clinician with a friendly, direct tone: you're here because you care about your health and you want practical steps you can take. If you have a condition that requires ongoing management, state your goals plainly: a plan that works in your daily life, an explanation you can repeat back to your family, and a timeline for follow-up testing or referrals. Your words matter, and your tone matters more—the confidence you project can influence how seriously your concerns are taken.

During the visit, keep a small audio note or a quick written record for yourself. If you're comfortable with it, ask to use the teach-back approach: after the doctor explains something, restate it in your own words and ask them to confirm. If a test is recommended, ask what the test will show, what the potential risks or limitations are, and what the next steps will look like. If a medication is prescribed, request a clear explanation of how it helps, what the side effects might be, and how to monitor its effectiveness. If the doctor uses a term you don't know, pause the moment with a light, honest request: *Could you spell that or explain it in simple terms?* You deserve to understand—not to be spoon-fed jargon in a language you don't speak fluently.

Structure your time by setting boundaries with kindness. If you sense a clinician is rushing you or brushing aside a concern, you can gracefully slow them down with a few phrases: *I'd like to understand this thoroughly before we move on, I need to know how this decision will affect my daily life,* or *What are the alternatives if this option doesn't feel right for me?* If the appointment is ending with more questions than answers, don't hesitate to request a follow-up or a phone call with a nurse or care coordinator who can walk you through the plan step by step. And if the vibe you're getting is *this is not your business*, remember you have a right to speak with a supervisor or to switch providers if necessary.

Finally, close with purpose. Leave the visit with a written summary of what was discussed, any orders or referrals, the exact next steps, and the names of who to contact if questions arise. If you're given a prescription, write the exact dosage and timing on your notes, and note any questions for your pharmacist. If a follow-up is required, mark it in your calendar, set reminders, and arrange a way to receive results without chasing them down later. You went in for care, and you deserve care that respects your time, your experience, and your life outside the clinic walls. That is your armor: preparedness, clarity, and a touch of humor to remind you that you are still the author of your own health story.

So breathe, straighten your shoulders, and remember this: you do not need a marching band to validate your concerns. You simply need to show up, be present, and claim the right to understand—and to be understood in return. The appointment is not a battle; it's a partnership, and you're walking in with the very best gear you've got: your voice, your records, and a plan you can live with.

TRANSLATING MEDICAL-ESE INTO HUMAN

What if you could turn the moment the doctor drops a term like "arterial Doppler" into a sentence you actually understand before the coffee goes cold in the waiting room? You can. The trick isn't shouting louder; it's translating the language of medicine into plain English you can own—and then using that understanding to guide your choices with confidence. This is your human translator moment, and yes, it comes with a few simple scripts and a lot of practical curiosity.

Start with the most basic goal: clarity. When you hear a term you don't know, pause for a beat and say, *Could you explain in plain language what that means for me?* Don't worry about sounding simple; you'll sound sane, thoughtful, and in charge. If the clinician uses an acronym or a test name, ask what it stands for, what it measures, and why it matters for your health now. For example, if a provider mentions an MRI, you can respond with a quick, *What will the MRI show, what are the risks, and what would be the next steps depending on the results?* It's a short, direct way to push the conversation toward actionable information rather than leaving you with more questions than answers.

Use the teach-back technique as your steady companion. Teach back means you restate the essential points in your own words and invite the clinician to correct any misunderstandings. It sounds simple, and it works, because it gives the doctor the opportunity to catch miscommunications before they become real problems. You might say, *Let me see if I've got this right: we're going to monitor blood pressure every visit for the next three months, adjust the dose if it stays high, and you'll check in with a follow-up phone call to discuss how I'm feeling? Is that accurate?* If the response tells you something unexpected, you've caught a potential misalignment early—and that's a win you can take to your kitchen table with a sigh of relief.

When it comes to tests and procedures, the person in the white coat often becomes a guide through a fog of numbers and probabilities. Ask about what the test is measuring and why it's the right choice for your body at this moment. If the explanation drifts into probability language, press gently for the practical implications: *What would a positive result mean for my day-to-day life? How might this change the plan we follow if results are normal or abnormal?* And remember, you are allowed to set boundaries around information you don't need right now. It's perfectly okay to say, *I'd rather not discuss radiology details unless it's essential to my immediate decision. Let's focus on what I need to do next week.*

A lot of medical jargon hides behind certainty. Your job is to strip that certainty down to usefulness. If a clinician says something like, *this is a standard precaution*, ask, *What does "standard" mean in this case? How does it apply to me? What are the alternatives if I want to explore more conservative options first?* You deserve to understand not just what is recommended, but why it is the recommended path for your unique circumstances. And if the doctor's explanation relies on statistics or population risk rather than your life, bring it back to you with a simple question: *How would this decision affect my day tomorrow, and the week after?*

Remember to translate not only words but expectations. If the appointment is framed around a single solution—one pill, one procedure—check in with your own values. You are not a walking chart; you are a person with a life that will be affected by every choice made in a clinic. It's your right to ask whether there are lifestyle or nonpharmacologic options that could work as well, or even better, before stepping into a heavy intervention.

If you feel the conversation slipping into a maze, bring it back with a guiding question that anchors the plan: *What are the three most important decisions we need to make today, and what does success look like if we make them together?* The clinician may provide an answer in medical language, and then you'll translate it into a plan that belongs in your world—one that you can explain to your sister, your grandchild, or your own reflection in the mirror without needing a translation app.

In the end, it's not about mastering every term; it's about mastering the moment. You're building a bridge from medical language to practical, everyday life. You're ensuring that decisions honor your goals, your energy, and your independence. Keep a small glossary in your head—not of terms you can't pronounce, but of questions you can always fall back on: What does this mean for me? How would this change my daily routine? What are the risks, the benefits, and the alternatives? And above all, can you walk me through it once more, so I can hear it and own it? That ownership is the real medicine.

MEDICATIONS, SUPPLEMENTS, AND THE KITCHEN COUNTER PHARMACY

If your kitchen counter could talk, it would likely say: I'm your most loyal, least fashionable pharmacist, and I am absolutely full of opinions. My spices are sunlit reminders of better days, and my bottles are evidence that aging is not a mystery to be solved but a system to be managed. Welcome to the kitchen counter pharmacy, where the shelves hold not just remedies but a daily ritual of self-advocacy. This is the place where you take charge of what you're taking and how you're taking it, so you don't become a walking pharmacy hazard with a dizzying side of confusion. Here's how to turn your counter into a clear, manageable, and even comedic ally that keeps you safe and sane.

The backbone of this system is a master list. You want one up-to-date roster that includes the medication's name, dosage, frequency, and purpose. It's not enough to know you're "on something for my heart" or that you "take a pill in the morning." You want the exact name (preferably both brand and generic), the exact dose, the exact time of day, and why you're taking it. When you see the doctor, bring this list and the actual bottles if possible. The goal is to prevent drug interactions, duplicate therapies, and the dreaded situation where you're taking a vitamin that cancels out a prescription or a supplement that triggers a side effect you don't like. If you're unsure whether something is a supplement, a vitamin, or a medication, treat it like a potential interaction and ask about it before you combine it with anything else.

Next comes the routine of tracking. Every

time you take a pill or a supplement, you add a tiny tick to your mental page, or better yet, to a small notebook or a simple app. Note the reason you're taking it and any effects you notice, good or bad. If a new symptom pops up after starting a drug or supplement, you've already got the data you need to discuss it with your clinician, instead of playing guessing games in the middle of the night. It's not about perfection; it's about clarity. Keep your medication in clearly labeled containers with the dosing schedule visible. If you have a spouse, caregiver, or grandchild who helps you, share access to the list so they can remind you if you forget. The more eyes you have, the safer you are.

The supplements deserve their own spotlight because they too live on the kitchen counter with a sense of entitlement. Vitamin D, magnesium, fish oil, herbal remedies—they all claim a place at the table. You want to note when you started each supplement, the dose, the brand if possible, and the reason. Do not assume that "natural" means safe. Some supplements can affect blood pressure, anticoagulant therapy, or how your body processes other medications. When you're unsure, your first question should be to your pharmacist or clinician, who can help you separate placebo from real benefit and identify interactions you might not foresee.

There's also the practical side of storage and disposal. Keep medications away from moisture and heat; avoid bathroom cabinets where toothpaste and steam can tax their stability. Rotate bottles so you don't forget you already took your morning pill, and set reminders if your memory isn't dependable in the moment. For old or unused medications, follow your local guidelines for disposal—do not flush them down the sink or toss them carelessly in the trash. Treat the disposal process with the same respect you give to your health care: a small ritual that keeps you safe and responsible.

What happens when a prescription changes? When a clinician adjusts a dose or switches a medication, update your list immediately and record the reason for the change. If you're taking multiple medicines, you might be tempted to shrug and say, *it's probably fine*, but the truth is that even small changes can ripple into new side effects, interactions, or energy shifts. Your future self will thank you for the meticulous note-taking you did today. You're not turning into a control freak; you're turning into the person who can actually make sense of their own body and its stories.

There's a quiet joy in turning responsibility into rhythm. The kitchen counter becomes a daily ritual rather than a battlefield. You celebrate simple wins: you didn't double-dose, you caught a potential interaction early, you asked a clarifying question and got a plain-language answer you could repeat to a friend. And yes, humor helps. When the bottle label uses more abbreviations than a tech manual, you pause, look up the plain language interpretation, and say to yourself, *I've earned the right to read this like a chapter from a favorite novel, not a legal brief.* This is where self-care meets practicality with a wink of humor—where a well-organized list becomes a map you can trust.

The kitchen counter pharmacy is not about perfection; it's about clarity, safety, and freedom. You deserve to know what's in your body's story and why it's there. You deserve to manage your medications in a way that respects your life and your energy—not an endless cycle of confusion, miscommunication, and mistaken doses. So set up your system, keep it current, and remember that every update is a small victory. You're building resilience one bottle, one dose, one note at a time—and you're doing it with the kind of steady humor that makes aging a little brighter and a lot more manageable.

WHEN YOU FEEL DISMISSED

You know that moment when you sense a doctor's tone slide from professional to dismissive, as if your concerns were an optional add-on to a ride you didn't actually want to take? If you've ever left a visit feeling smaller than your health concerns, you're not imagining the experience. Dismissal can be subtle—a shrug, a sigh, a quick change of topic—or it can be loud, a moment where your age becomes the excuse for not listening. This chapter isn't about angering anyone; it's about reclaiming your voice, your agency, and the right to be taken seriously, even when the situation feels like a medical labyrinth. Here are practical scripts, strategies, and a path to better care without turning a routine appointment into a confrontation.

First, set your boundary before you even step in. Remind yourself that your concerns are legitimate, that you deserve respectful listening, and that you're there to collaborate on a plan that works for you. If you hear a dismissive line, respond with a calm clarity: *I understand your perspective, but my concern is real and I'd like to address it now rather than later.* If the clinician Minimizes or shifts away from the issue, gently pivot back with a specific request: *I'd like to discuss X in detail and see possible options for managing it today.* If you're not comfortable with the pace or the approach, you can invite a nurse, another clinician, or a patient advocate to join the conversation, emphasizing that you value collaboration and want the best outcome for your health.

A powerful tool in the moment is to ask for a concrete plan. If you're told that something is "not urgent," you can ask, *What would make this urgent for me? What specific signs or symptoms should prompt a follow-up, and when would you want to see me again?* People respect decisiveness when it's paired with a reasonable timeline. If you're offered only a vague next step, request a written plan or a patient portal note that outlines the decisions, options, and next steps. A written plan isn't a black-box—it's a roadmap that you can return to when memory, fatigue, or life gets loud.

If you still feel dismissed after attempting to engage, you have boundaries you can enforce. You can explicitly request a referral to a different clinician who can give you the attention you deserve, or you can contact the clinic's patient relations or care coordination department for guidance. When you explain your experience, use concrete facts and impact rather than general frustration. For example, *During the visit, I mentioned persistent muscle pain and sleep disruption, and I didn't feel the explanation acknowledged the impact these symptoms have on my daily life. I'm asking for a fuller assessment or a referral to someone who can help me manage these symptoms more effectively.* It's a sentence that states the problem and your need without drama, preserving your dignity and your energy.

Sometimes the most powerful approach is to shift the relationship, not the room. Schedule a follow-up with a clinician who has a track record of listening, or consider bringing a trusted companion to the visit who can help you articulate concerns and serve as a memory aid. If you're consistently met with resistance from a particular provider, you may decide to switch clinics or request a doctor who specializes in geriatric care or patient-centered communication. You aren't being a troublemaker; you're seeking accountability and compassionate care that respects your life story as much as your lab results.

Operating from a stance of informed readiness reduces the sting of being dismissed. When you walk away with a plan, a documented discussion, and a clear path forward, you've already won half the battle. You've preserved your dignity, and you've safeguarded your health. And if you need a reminder, give yourself a tiny celebration for daring to demand better care: a favorite treat, a phone call to a friend, or a little victory dance in the hallway to remind yourself that you are not invisible.

THE WAITING ROOM COMEDY HOUR

If you've ever spent a long afternoon in the waiting room, you know it's less a waiting room and more a stage where everyone is auditioning for the next act in a life that's already interesting enough. The chairs squeak, the magazine shuffle is relentless, and the clock seems to run on a separate, slower metronome. Yet the waiting room is not just a pit stop; it's an opportunity to stretch your patience, sharpen your humor, and set yourself up for a smoother motion through the rest of the day. This chapter invites you to reframe the space as your own mini-retreat where you practice calm, connection, and a dash of mischief to keep your spirits high as the minutes tick by.

Begin with a mindset switch. Instead of seeing the waiting room as a delay, see it as a chance to ground yourself. Take a slow, deliberate breath in, count to four, and exhale for four. Repeat a couple of times, noticing the rise and fall of your chest, the rhythm of your heartbeat, the way your shoulders drop a notch with each exhale. If you're anxious, bring a tiny comfort object or a photo that reminds you of a happy moment. If you're bored, allow yourself to observe kindly—the quiet rituals of others waiting, the small acts of kindness from staff, the way a child's laughter leaks through a door and reminds you what joy sounds like.

Have a few coping tricks ready that don't rely on technology or loud sounds. Bring a book that makes you smile rather than one that requires heavy thinking. A notebook to jot quick reflections or a few lines of gratitude can transform the moment into a creative pause instead of a drain. Small talk with the person in the chair next to you can provide a moment of human connection, or you can simply watch the world go by and notice the tiny details—the patient's scarf that matches the nurse's scrubs, the way the receptionist types with a rhythm that becomes oddly comforting, the wall art that tries its best to be optimistic no matter the hour. Humor, of course, is your reliable ally. If someone shares a dramatic health tale, you can respond with warmth and levity: *We're going to keep a whole library of good-news stories today, and you're the opening chapter!* It's a light, friendly line that acknowledges the moment without turning it into a spectacle.

If delays sneak up on you, use the time to reinforce your own boundaries and independence. Gather your thoughts, scan your questions, and review your appointment goals. The waiting room offers a chance to practice the exact conversation you want to have with your clinician, so when you finally reach the exam room, you're not off balance—you're grounded and ready. Keep a mental note of any recurring frustrations and store them as feedback for the clinic, not as fuel for your own frustration. Good clinics want to hear how the experience can improve, and your constructive feedback can help shape better care for others who come after you.

And then there's the moment you leave. You walk out with your head high, a plan in your pocket, and the feeling that you've spent an afternoon not simply waiting but gathering strength. The waiting room becomes a ritual of resilience, a place to demonstrate to yourself that time can be used wisely even when the clock seems to have paused just for you. Humor remains your most reliable tool—an understated joke about the length of a magazine article, a wink at the nurse who hands you the door key with a friendly salute. You leave not defeated by delay but empowered by your ability to navigate it with grace and grit. That is the real reward of the Waiting Room Comedy Hour: a reminder that you're still the lead in your own life, even when the script includes a few extra lines from the universe about patience.

FOUR
MENOPAUSE'S LINGERING CAMEOS (AND OTHER HORMONAL AFTER-PARTIES)

HOT FLASHES: NATURE'S PERSONAL SAUNA

If menopause had a business card, it would read always on, occasionally dramatic, and forever testing the air conditioning in your own body. Hot flashes arrive like uninvited guests who insist on staying for the after party and leaving the thermostat in a new, unpredictable place. One minute you are calmly sipping tea, the next you are a portable radiator that can't decide between sweating through your blouse or inflating a fan club for your own shoulders. The good news is you are not alone, and you can ride this heat wave with wit, a little strategy, and clothing that behaves like a tactical armor rather than a hair dryer you forgot to switch off.

Temperature tantrums are less about willpower and more about physiology doing a dramatic improv piece. Your brain sends a signal to your blood vessels to widen, your heart rate climbs, and suddenly your body becomes a tiny steam engine in a linen shirt. Triggers vary from caffeine to spicy foods, stress to sudden changes in room temperature, and yes, even the moment you walk into a store and realize the air conditioning is enviably enthusiastic. The basic rule is to prepare rather than panic. Think layers that work like a weather system you can control. Start with a breathable base layer that wicks moisture, add a mid layer you can peel off without a detour to the emergency room, and finish with a cardigan or jacket you can fling to the side with theatrical flair when the flash hits mid conversation.

Wardrobe is part armor, part drama club. Lightweight fabrics like cotton and bamboo stay cool, while tiny details can save you from an accidental sauna effect. A cooling scarf, a compact handheld fan, or a small cooling towel tucked in your tote can transform a public episode into a quick reset. Keep a cold bottle of water handy and sip regularly; hydration matters more than you realize. Cold foods and drinks can offer immediate relief, but staying hydrated through the day keeps the baseline from sliding into lava status. And yes, you will learn the art of strategic fan placement: aim the breeze where it helps most, not where people pretend to be impressed by your own personal climate control.

Practical routines work wonders. In the mornings, do a quick check in with your body. If you wake to a dim fog of heat, one gentle stretch, a glass of water, and a cool shower can set a calmer tone for the day. Throughout the day, keep snacks that stabilize energy and blood sugar handy; blood sugar dips can worsen heat sensations and mood swings, so a small handful of nuts or a piece of fruit can feel heroic. Exercise plays a crucial role too, not as punishment but as a tool that trains your system to manage heat better. A brisk walk, a short cycle, or even a dance in your living room improves circulation and gives you a sense of agency when the storm starts.

There is purpose in the discomfort. Hot

flashes are not just an inconvenience; they are a reminder that your body is in a powerful transition, learning how to regulate itself in a new way. That learning might come with moments of embarrassment, but it also brings opportunities for self care you did not know you needed. When you treat hot flashes as a signal rather than a fault, you reclaim a level of control that can feel surprisingly liberating. And while you cannot predict every episode, you can predict your response, and that is where the real power lies. As you sharpen your toolkit, you will find yourself cooler not just in temperature but in spirit, ready to handle the next cameo with a smile and a shrug that says I got this.

In the pages ahead, you will discover strategies that blend practicality with humor, turning each heat moment into a plot twist you can gently steer. The next section dives into mood and the elusive is it me question, because hormonal tides do not stop at the surface; they rummage through every room in your mind and demand a response that is honest, kind, and entirely yours to craft.

MOOD, ANXIETY, AND THE IS IT ME QUESTION

Have you ever wondered whether your mood is a personal weather pattern or a subscription you forgot you signed up for? Mood in this chapter is not a dramatic diva to be shushed but a rowdy chorus in the background of your day. Hormones can rewrite the score with surprising speed, turning a peaceful morning into a roller coaster and a simple text message into a day altering mystery. The moment you notice you are riding a mood wave you did not authorize, remember this is not a defect in character; it is a natural part of a changing hormonal landscape. The question Is it me or is it something else becomes a safety check you can run without shame or self blame.

Pattern spotting is the first step toward regaining agency. Keep a simple log for a couple of weeks: note what time you wake, what you ate, your caffeine intake, how much sleep you got, any notable stressors, and how you felt on a scale from 1 to 10 at several points during the day. You will start to see a map appear. Perhaps irritability spikes after a caffeine surge, or sleep fragmentation mirrors a daytime fog; maybe heavy meals kick off a crash of low energy and crankiness. This is not a guilt trip; it is data that helps you respond instead of react. With data in hand, you can plan adjustments that protect your mood without asking you to become someone you are not.

Support is not a sign of weakness but a smart strategy. Talk to someone you trust about the way you are feeling and how it might be connected to sleep, heat, or general life stress. A trusted friend, family member, or neighbor can help you navigate the calmer moments and the rough patches with more ease. If mood shifts begin to overshadow daily life — if you notice persistent sadness, anxiety that freezes you in place, or thoughts that feel unmoored from reality — it is time to seek professional help. You deserve a space where you can say the words you are afraid to say out loud without feeling like you are overreacting.

Therapy can be a powerful ally on this journey, and you do not have to commit to a lifetime of weekly sessions to gain value. Short term counseling, support groups, or an appointment with a clinician who understands menopause can provide tools to handle rumination, anxiety, and the burden of second guessing yourself. If you are comfortable exploring medical options you may discuss how hormone changes intersect with mood and sleep. Some women find benefit in targeted treatments under medical supervision, while others thrive with non medical approaches such as mindfulness, movement, and structured routines. Either path you choose, the aim is the same: to move from constant reconsideration to confident decision making.

The true aim here is not to erase all emotion but to tune it so you can show up for the life you want. When you feel a little steadier, you can face the world with the same humor you bring to a late bus or a long line at the grocery store. The next section shifts toward the skin and moisture questions that accompany this stage of life, because when your outer shell changes, your daily routine needs to adapt without losing its sparkle.

SKIN, HAIR, AND THE NEW RULES OF MOISTURE

Your skin has moved from a smooth, responsive canvas to a landscape where moisture is a scarce resource and elasticity is a learned skill. It is easy to panic when you notice fine lines developing or your cheekbones that once felt sunlit now show their backstage shadows. But this is not a crisis; it is a cosmetic climate change, and you are the seasoned traveler who knows how to pack wisely. The new rules of moisture are not about turning every morning into a spa ritual; they are about creating a simple, sustainable routine that respects your skin's new tempo.

The dryness you notice is often the most obvious sign of change, but it hides a larger story about how your skin holds onto moisture, what irritates it, and what helps it stay resilient. Start with a gentle cleanse that respects the barrier rather than stripping it away. Choose a cleanser that is mild and fragrance free, avoiding harsh detergents that can feel like a wake up call to your skin each morning. Follow with a moisturizer that features ceramides or glycerin; these ingredients help lock in moisture and support the barrier you depend on for comfort and protection. A sunscreen with broad spectrum coverage becomes less optional and more of a daily ritual, a shield that keeps your face from becoming a map of sun exposure and cumulative aging.

Texture matters now more than ever. If your skin feels tight after washing, you have found your cue to switch to something richer but not heavy. Layering can be your friend: a lighter serum on top of your moisturizer can offer a hydration boost without feeling greasy. If retinoids interest you, start slowly and see how your skin responds, because the current climate may require more patience with peak results. Hydration is not only external; internal hydration matters as well. Keep water within reach, and if you notice hair feeling rough or dry, adjust your routine with a gentle shampoo and a conditioner that restores shine without weighing you down. For hair color, consider whether you want to embrace natural gray or continue with a color that suits your vibe; either choice can be fabulous, as long as you feel comfortable in your own skin.

A few practical routines can simplify life without sacrificing results. A quick morning ritual that includes a gentle cleanse, a light layer of moisturizer with SPF, and a touch of color for a fresh look can set the tone for the day. At night, a slightly richer moisturizer or a thin layer of oil can seal in moisture while you sleep, allowing your skin to recover during those hours when regeneration happens most naturally. Sun protection remains a non negotiable habit, weather beaming sun or sneaking through clouds; a broad SPF every day keeps the long term risks at bay and the complexion more even. As you adjust to your skin's new cadence, you will notice not only the comfort but the confidence that comes from honoring what your body needs rather than fighting against it.

The head and the scalp share in this update, with hair that may feel coarser, finer, or simply different in texture. You may notice changes in volume, curl pattern, or how your hair holds color. Gentle care is essential here as well. Avoid aggressive heat styling and consider a light styling product that adds grip without weighing you down. If gray roots are making a bold statement you did not plan on, invest in a look that feels intentional. You are not aging into invisibility; you are redefining how you present the you that remains excited by life. The next part of this chapter turns toward a different kind of intimacy—the practical, emotional, and physical terrain of connection and closeness.

INTIMACY AND COMFORT

Romance after 60 does not vanish; it often mutates into a form that requires cleverness, humor, and honest conversation. You may find that arousal, sensitivity, and comfort shift in surprising ways, and this is not a sign to retire your love life but a cue to renegotiate how you experience closeness. If you have faced vaginal dryness or discomfort during intimacy, know that you are not alone and you are not broken. A simple, reliable approach is to experiment with lubricants that are water based or silicone based, avoiding products with fragrances or irritants. Lubricants can transform a moment that used to feel effortless into a shared, relaxed experience, reducing friction and increasing pleasure. If you use latex condoms, choose lubricants compatible with latex and be mindful of any sensitivities. You deserve to feel comfortable advocating for your needs, not shrinking around them.

Communication becomes the cornerstone

of intimacy in this phase. A gentle, honest conversation with your partner about what feels good, what hurts, and what would make the moment easier can deepen trust and connection. It may also reveal that you can reshape your relationship in small, meaningful ways. Foreplay, eye contact, and touch that emphasizes emotional closeness often matter more than a long, complicated sexual routine. The energy you have for intimacy can vary from day to day, so recognizing energy patterns and planning around them helps you maintain a sense of control rather than letting the situation control you.

In addition to lubricants and conversation, consider addressing the practical side of intimacy: comfort in bed and sleep quality can influence arousal and mood. Adjust bedding to cooler fabrics, use breathable cotton sheets, and ensure the room temperature supports a calm start to the night. Simple routines, such as shared winding down time with a light conversation or a favorite show, can maintain closeness even on days when energy is low. You may also explore additional options like pelvic floor exercises that promote strength and circulation, which can contribute to greater sensation and comfort. The key is to view intimacy as a living practice that evolves with you, not as a box to check off. The next section covers a different kind of important conversation—when to seek professional guidance beyond the DIY tips and home remedies.

WHEN TO TALK TO A PROFESSIONAL

If your body is sending warning flags, it is not an act of melodrama to listen closely. It is a sign that your health deserves attention, care, and a serious dose of reassurance. So when should you pick up the phone or make an appointment? There are certain signals that you should not ignore. If mood changes become persistent, if sleep is broken beyond repair, if anxiety or irritability feels unmanageable, or if you experience days where daily tasks feel impossible, these are red flags worth professional evaluation. If you notice significant weight changes, recurring headaches that refuse to fade, chest pain, shortness of breath, or heavy vaginal bleeding that is new or worsening, contact a clinician promptly. These symptoms call for medical advice rather than a DIY Rube Goldberg machine of home remedies, no matter how confident you are in your ability to handle life on your own.

Preparation helps you get the most from medical visits. Start a symptom diary for at least two weeks, noting when issues occur, how long they last, what preceded them, and how they respond to simple interventions. Bring a list of medications, supplements, and any other therapies you are trying, including herbal remedies, as these can interact with conventional treatments in surprising ways. If you have a primary care provider who is not specialized in menopause yet, ask for a referral to a gynecologist, an endocrinologist, or a menopause clinic with experience in midlife health. These specialists can offer options that are tailored to your physiology and your life goals.

Conversations with healthcare professionals are not about surrender; they are about sovereignty over your body. You deserve clear explanations, honest assessments, and choices that align with your priorities. This might include local estrogen therapy for vaginal dryness, certain hormone therapies if appropriate, or non hormone approaches that focus on sleep, mood, and energy. It is also perfectly valid to seek mental health support if mood, anxiety, or grief feels overwhelming. A clinician can help you navigate the emotional terrain with evidence based guidance and compassionate listening. You do not have to face the hormonal after party alone; you can invite professionals to help you choreograph a plan that respects your autonomy while offering the support you deserve.

As you close this chapter, remember that knowledge plus humor equals resilience. The goal is not to pretend that changes do not exist but to approach them with practical strategies and a sense of play. You have earned the right to live on your own terms, to laugh at the moments that try to steal your spotlight, and to keep steering your life toward joy, connection, and vitality. The chapter may end here, but your new season is only just beginning, and you deserve to step forward with confidence, curiosity, and a little mischief in your pocket.

FIVE
RETIREMENT REINVENTION—NOW WHAT DO I DO ALL DAY?

THREE-MONTH RESET: REST WITHOUT RETREAT

Retirement isn't a permanent vacation; it's a choose-your-own-adventure with more naps. If you're waking up each morning thinking you should be busier because you've earned your leisure, you're not alone. The truth is gentler: rest is not a reward for hard work; it's the fuel for whatever you want to do next. The first ninety days after stepping off the clock should feel a little like wandering through a sunlit mall you've never explored before—lots of doors, some you'll love, some you'll skip, and a lot of discovering what feels good when you're not rushing to clock in. The goal isn't to fill every hour with something shiny, but to design a rhythm that returns energy you didn't realize you misplaced during your career years.

Picture this: the first week you slowly peel away the to-do lists that used to own you, replacing them with tiny, welcoming rituals. A morning ritual might be a longer stretch in bed followed by a cup of coffee that doesn't come with a deadline. Perhaps a Sunday afternoon walk with a notebook to jot down ideas that drift in from nowhere—ideas you'll later decide are worth chasing or worth yawning at. The calendar, once a battlefield of deadlines, becomes a playground where you get to test-drive different moods.

The first nonnegotiable of these ninety days is decompression with intention. You don't disappear; you reappear to yourself. You permit yourself to do nothing in the way that feels like something, to savor the quiet, to notice the little things—a neighbor's lilac bush, a bar of chocolate that tastes different when you don't have a meeting hanging over your head. The second nonnegotiable is gentle exposure to the world you're about to inhabit. You dip a toe into a class, a club, or a volunteer gig not as a test but as an invitation to explore. The third nonnegotiable is a real, warm boundary around time. You guard your mornings or your afternoons as if you were protecting something fragile—because you are protecting your future energy for the life you want to live.

In practice, this might look like one regular, low-pressure activity per week, scheduled at the same time, so it becomes part of your routine rather than a rescue mission when you're already exhausted. It might be a one-hour Zumba class that ends with a giggle at your own balance, or a monthly coffee with a friend who gets you without needing a PowerPoint on how you're spending your time. And for those days when the couch is a better confidant than any committee chair, you allow it. You learn to distinguish between rest that restores and rest that becomes an escape hatch from life.

Why does this matter? Because the myth that retirement is nothing but endless leisure can hollow you out faster than a stale bread loaf. Rest is the glue that holds your next chapters together. With a three-month reset, you're not just surviving the transition—you're setting a stage where meaningful pursuits can land with less drama and more delight. You'll wake up feeling curious instead of obligated, hopeful instead of overwhelmed, and ready to say yes to opportunities that align with who you are today, not who you were yesterday.

As you ease into this phase, you'll start noticing what actually recharges you. Maybe it's time spent with a grandchild building a cardboard spaceship; maybe it's a quiet afternoon of painting or gardening, or perhaps it's hosting a book club where you read aloud and listen more than you talk. The point is not to force a new identity overnight but to allow layers to reveal themselves, slowly and with humor. And if a misstep happens—if you overcommit to a charity gala you don't enjoy or you realize a hobby you loved five years ago now feels like work—you'll pause, adjust, and laugh at yourself. After all, reinvention isn't a sprint; it's a comedy of trials, errors, and occasional triumphs.

So let the first ninety days be a warm introduction to the life you're about to redesign. The chapters ahead will ask you to guard your time, to lean into joy, and to test the boundaries of your own independence. You'll discover that rest can be a radical act, that silence can host ideas, and that the best version of you is not the one who pretends to be busy, but the one who chooses what truly matters—and does so with a grin. What new morning routines will you try first, and which ones will get folded into your personal rhythm without apology?

WHO AM I WITHOUT THE JOB TITLE?

What if tomorrow you introduced yourself not as a former executive, nurse, teacher, or manager but simply as a human with a good laugh and a long list of incomplete crafts? Identity after the job title is the quiet art of reclaiming who you are beyond the badge you wore for decades. It's less about erasing memory and more about reimagining it as a foundation, not a ceiling. The moment you step away from the job, you may notice your sense of self slipping into a curious fog—one that asks for a fresh reference point, a new nameplate on the door you open every morning. The fog is not a failure; it's a doorway. And the doorway is wide enough for a hundred versions of you, each one more surprising than the last.

Here's a truth worth repeating: your worth isn't tied to a paycheck or a position. It's tied to your presence, your choices, and the way you make people feel when you walk into a room with your particular blend of wit and warmth. To begin rewriting your identity, start with a simple inventory of what still lights you up. Think of five roles you've always wanted to explore beyond your career—mentor, traveler, storyteller, gardener, neighbor, tutor, artist, organizer, or volunteer. Then give each role a small test drive. Spend an afternoon teaching a neighbor how to use a smartphone camera. Sign up for a three-week pottery class and see if the clay becomes clay or a diary you keep in your hands. Try hosting a monthly potluck where you bring a dish you've never cooked before, and see how it feels to be the organizer rather than the guest who is served. The goal isn't to become someone new overnight; it's to let the facets you set aside during professional life find space to breathe again.

What often trips people up is the belief that change must be dramatic to count. In reality, it's the countless tiny affirmations that accumulate into a new you. You may begin to notice that your confidence comes from choosing what you want to do and when you want to do it, rather than from doing what someone else thinks you should. Your phrasing matters too. Instead of saying I am retired or I am slowing down, try I am choosing to devote time to what matters most. I am learning what brings me joy and what drains me. I am designing days that fit who I am now. Those small, honest statements are powerful identity anchors.

As you craft a new sense of self, keep the door open to change. Some days you'll slip back into old roles with affection and humor, and that's okay. The aim is not perfection but permission: permission to redefine yourself on your own terms. You might discover that part of your new identity is simply being honest about what you don't want anymore and brave enough to say no. And when you share this evolving self with others, you'll notice a surprising thing: people want to hear about your evolving life because it feels real and human, not polished and performative.

What's one activity you've been too afraid to try because you fear it will redefine you in unexpected ways? What would your five new roles look like when tested in small, joyful experiments?

THE FUN BUDGET AND THE NO-THANKS BUDGET

Time, like money, is a resource you get to allocate with intention. The Fun Budget is the portion you set aside specifically for joy, curiosity, and activities that light you up. The No-Thanks Budget is the opposite side of the coin: the boundaries you draw around what you won't do or who you won't become when someone asks for your energy and time. Treat these as two halves of a humane, generous approach to retirement—one that honors your needs without turning you into a martyr for other people's expectations.

Let me tell you about a Sunday I spent with my own Fun Budget intact. I woke up without an alarm and brewed a pot of coffee that tasted like a vacation. I pulled a sketchbook from the back of a cabinet I hadn't opened in years, and I doodled silly flowers that looked more like friendly amoebas than anything worthy of an art show. The joy wasn't in the outcome but the permission to indulge in a tiny block of time devoted to nothing but play. Later, I met a friend for a casual lunch, and we wandered through a store where we laughed at items we would never buy but enjoyed pretending to debate. That day cost me less than a typical day out, but it filled the hours with something that felt like a gift rather than an obligation.

The No-Thanks Budget works like a friendly filter. It's the practice of saying no to invites that drain your energy, politely and firmly, so you can say yes to the ones that nourish you. It's about avoiding the trap of perpetual guilt—the nagging sense that if you don't show up, you're letting someone down. You're not letting anyone down when you protect what makes you feel alive. You're honoring the fact that your time is finite and your enthusiasm is precious. This boundary is not a wall; it's a doorway to calmer days and clearer choices.

The practical trick here is to attach both

budgets to a simple ritual: a weekly planning moment. Sit with a notebook, a calendar, and a pen that actually glides. Ask yourself what would spark real joy this week and what would drain you in a way that's not worth the cost. If the answer is a heart sink rather than a spark, cross it off with a flourish. If the answer is yes, you write it down and commit to it with a clear time block. The power comes from consistency. Your Fun Budget grows not by grand gestures but by repeated, small acts of choosing pleasure on purpose.

Remember: you are not avoiding life by saying no to certain things. You are creating space for the things that make life feel like you, not a version of you someone else designed. What would a balanced Fun Budget look like for you this month, and what No-Thanks moments would you gladly reclaim without apology?

VOLUNTEERING, CLASSES, AND PART-TIME WORK

If retirement has a mood, it's this: meaningful options without burnout, connection without chaos, and the occasional paycheck that reminds you you still have skills worth sharing. The right path isn't a single road but a mosaic made of volunteering gigs, classes that spark curiosity, and part-time work that respects your energy. You're not chasing productivity trophies; you're collecting experiences that remind you you're still a contributor, still capable, and still in charge of how you spend your time.

Volunteering offers a particularly rich avenue for this era because it plugs you into community and gives you a fresh audience for your stories, your talents, and your patience. You might become a mentor at a local school, where the wisdom of your years lands on a student with a question you could answer in your sleep. Or you might volunteer at a museum or a library, where your knowledge about a certain period or craft becomes a doorway for others to walk through. The beauty of volunteering is that it's often flexible. You can choose a gig that requires a few hours a week or one that fits around a caregiving schedule. The payoff is not only in what you give but in what you receive—new friends, a renewed sense of purpose, and a reminder that your voice still matters.

Classes are a different kind of spark. They don't demand you become a novice forever; they invite you to become a student again, which is a surprisingly delightful stance to adopt in your sixties. A cooking course might teach you a sauce you'll brag about at family gatherings; a pottery class could give you a mug you'll insist is your own. A language lesson could unlock a conversation with a grandchild visiting from another country, adding a practical, heartwarming thread to your family tapestry. Part-time work, when chosen with care, offers a bridge between the social world of a job and the freedom you crave in retirement. Quick shifts—temp assistance at a bookstore, a receptionist role at a community center, a tutoring gig on weekends—keep you connected without demanding every hour.

One practical way to approach this is to treat volunteering, classes, and light work as a menu rather than a plan. Taste-test different options for a season, measure how they feel in your body and your schedule, and note the impact on sleep, mood, and social energy. If a suggested role leaves you depleted or anxious, that's information. If it feels exciting and sustaining, that's a signal to lean in a little longer. The right fit should feel like a warm invitation rather than a heavy obligation.

As you explore, you'll notice a pattern: meaningful work in this phase isn't about achieving a résumé milestone; it's about shaping a life where your presence matters. You'll see that your stories can guide others, your hands can create something tangible, and your time can be spent in ways that honor who you are now. The long game is not about proving yourself but about preserving your energy so you can laugh, learn, and contribute with a grin. What's one volunteering opportunity you've been curious about, and what's a small step you can take this week to test it?

A WEEK THAT FEELS LIKE YOURS

If retirement is a stage, this chapter is your rehearsal for a daily performance that fits you —no props required, just your own authenticity on a sunlit set. A week that feels like yours begins with the gentlest of awakenings. Imagine a morning that starts with a slow stretch and a cup of coffee that doesn't have to hurry you out the door. You linger with a book for ten minutes longer or you just sit, listening to the world wake up. Breakfast might be something comforting and simple, a ritual you can feel good about because it's nourishing rather than a scramble to chase the day. The aim is a pace that doesn't beat you to the punch.

On Monday, you try something small that's new: a class, a club, a chat with a neighbor about a shared interest. The aim is curiosity rather than commitment; you want to test-drive a feeling you've wanted to explore for months or years. Tuesday and Wednesday aren't about endless errands but about rhythm. A mid-morning walk, a short call with a friend who makes you laugh, a quiet afternoon in the kitchen experimenting with a recipe that ends with a clean counter and a grin. You pencil in a longer activity for the week—perhaps a volunteer shift, a library lecture, or a visit to a gallery—yet you keep it low-key, so your energy has room to breathe.

By Thursday you notice your energy patterns: you're not counting every minute; you're listening to how your body responds to different tasks. If a social commitment feels heavy, you rearrange it for another day or decline with a lighthearted note that keeps the door open. Friday becomes your celebration day—an opportunity to gather with friends, indulge in a favorite hobby, or simply float through the evening with a movie that makes you sigh with contentment instead of stress. The weekend is a blend of rest and play, with room for spontaneity. Maybe you take a short road trip, or you invite the grandkids over for a project that becomes part of your shared story.

A week that feels like you also requires a practical architecture. You'll want a reliable rhythm for meals, sleep, and movement that respects your energy while leaving space for joy. A sunrise or early morning ritual can bookend your days with intention, while a late afternoon walk can help you digest both the day's affairs and the day's laughter. You'll design the week with a simple calendar—one recurring event like a weekly stroll, one recurring social hour, and one flexible block where you can say yes to something that arises spontaneously without worrying about derailing your plan. The objective isn't to create a flawless schedule but to cultivate a living map that nods to your needs while inviting new experiences.

As you read this, you might think: this sounds nice, but what if life interrupts? The answer is simple: life will always interrupt. The beauty of a week that feels like yours is that it includes room for those interruptions, too. Your plan isn't a cage; it's a compass. It points you toward moments of calm, connection, and curiosity, and it reminds you that you still get to decide what fills your time. So, what would a single, ordinary week look like if you let it be remarkable in small, human ways? And what tiny change could you make this week to tilt the scales toward more of those moments?

SIX
FRIENDSHIP AFTER 60— YOUR CIRCLE, YOUR RULES

FRIENDSHIP DRIFT AND HOW NOT TO TAKE IT PERSONALLY

If you're reading this with a mug of tea that's gone cold because you've spent the last hour texting back a friend you haven't seen in six months, you know the truth already: friendship after sixty isn't a straight line. It's a winding country road with potholes you didn't see coming, detours you never planned for, and occasional vistas that remind you how beautiful this ride can be when you're not alone. The good news is that drift isn't a betrayal of your life's compass; it's a natural weather pattern in a life that's weathering, remodeling, and rediscovering itself. People move at different speeds now—retirements reshuffle priorities, families expand in surprising ways, and energy budgets require more careful planning than a grandchild's school concert schedule. So when a friendship feels distant, it isn't automatically a verdict on you. It can be a sign that you both need a new rhythm—and maybe a batch of your famous chocolate chip cookies to sweeten the transition.

Take the case of my neighbor, Ruth, who used to call every Sunday for a long, meandering chat about nothing and everything. Then Ruth joined a morning pickleball league that starts before the sun, and suddenly our Sunday ritual needed a new time slot. We drifted, not because we disliked each other, but because life got busy and our calendars stopped agreeing on a shared moment. Instead of circling the wagons in a dramatic confrontation, we did what grown people do when the weather changes: we talked, we adjusted, and we found a way to reconnect that actually fit. Our talks got shorter, but they carried more intention. We traded "What's new?" for "What's one small thing you're hoping for this month?" and the friendship found a gentler cadence. There's humor in realizing that you both still want each other in your lives, just on different pages of the same book.

So how do you respond kindly when a drift starts to feel personal? First, acknowledge the emotion without judging it. For a moment, name the hurt—"I feel a little tossed by the changing tides of our contact." Then switch to curiosity—"What was your week like? What's something that lights you up these days?" When you approach the situation with curiosity rather than accusation, you give the other person room to respond honestly without shutting down. And yes, you can be clear about what you need without turning it into a demand. You can say, *I'd love to keep in touch, even if it's a text once a week or a quick coffee catch-up every couple of weeks.* The key is to preserve your own energy while inviting theirs back into the orbit, not to force a return to a fictional past.

Another essential idea: boundaries aren't walls; they're gates with good hinges. A boundary says, in effect, "I value our friendship, and I also need space to live my life the way I'm living it now." Boundaries can be as simple as choosing the method and tempo of communication—text versus call, weekday versus weekend, short check-ins versus longer conversations. Boundaries can involve shared calendar moments—set a standing monthly brunch and a quarterly adventure—so you both show up with anticipation, not guilt. And boundaries aren't a one-time declaration. They're a practice, a routine you revisit as life does its inevitable zigzag.

There will be grieving moments too. Not every drift ends in fireworks and reconciliation; some fade with a soft, unspoken goodbye that feels equal parts relief and nostalgia. When that happens, give yourself permission to release with gratitude instead of bitterness. You can thank a friend for the good years, honor the laughter you shared, and still step forward without carrying a backpack full of guilt for someone else's pace.

Making peace with drift is a skill, not a license to cling to people who drain you. It's about honoring the people who matter while protecting the space in your life where joy, laughter, and your own voice have a right to show up loudly. If you can do that, your circle will feel less like a static ring and more like a living system—pulsing, evolving, and, yes, capable of surprising you in the best possible way. The goal isn't to chase every friendship back into perfect alignment; it's to curate a circle that honors both your history and your ongoing become. And that's how you turn drift into growth, one kind boundary, one renewed connection, and one well-timed snack at a time.

MAKING NEW FRIENDS WITHOUT FEELING LIKE A TRANSFER STUDENT

You'll know you're ready for new friendships when your heart is open to possibility but your brain has learned the comfort of night-and-day routine. After sixty, the fear of awkward first meetings is often the loudest voice in the room. You've mastered the art of carrying a conversation through a morning coffee without spilling it; you can negotiate a grocery list in a clinical, focused tone that would impress a doctor. Yet the moment you're asked, "Do you want to join this group?" your inner transfer student pops up, clutching a schedule and whispering, "Am I going to be the new kid again?" The good news is that new-friend magic isn't about being charming on cue; it's about showing up with your whole, imperfect, hilarious self and letting the right people catch the vibe.

First, pick a few venues where the chances of meeting like-minded people are higher than a lottery draw. Community centers and libraries run clubs that aren't swayed by trend; they're anchored in shared activities—book clubs, garden clubs, walking groups, and volunteer teams. If you're tech-curious like many of us, online communities rooted in real-life meetups can also be a bridge. The point is not to chase a million acquaintances but to cultivate a handful of connections that feel safe enough to test the waters with a joke and a listening ear. When you go to these places, bring one thing that feels you: a story, a recommendation, a snack, something you're not afraid to admit you love. People connect over specifics—the best kind of details that invite a genuine yes, I get you, and I'd like to hear more.

Then there's the art of the casual invitation. "Would you like to join me for a walk this Saturday morning?" lands differently than "We should hang out sometime." Treat every invitation like a small, precious asset you're willing to invest in. If someone says yes, celebrate with a small ritual—acknowledge the moment, remember a detail from your conversation, and plan a simple next step. It could be a second coffee, a shared recipe, or a stroll through a local market. If someone says no, give yourself space to feel the sting and then remind yourself that a rejection isn't a referendum on your worth; it's a misalignment of schedules, energy, or interests. And if the response is tepid, don't be discouraged. The right person might appear in the most unexpected place—a line at a farmers market, a neighbor's dog-walk conversation, or the person who always reaches for the same chair at your neighborhood book club.

Let's be practical about how to read social chemistry without a science degree. Focus on two or three qualities that feel non-negotiable for you: reciprocity, reliability, and shared values or humor. Reciprocity is the easiest to assess in the moment: do you feel a lift after you talk, or does every exchange feel like an obligation? Reliability is visible in the small things—shows up on time, keeps promises, responds with thoughtfulness rather than avoidance. Shared values or humor isn't a checklist; it's the sense that you both "get" the other person, you laugh at roughly the same things, and you can disagree with civility and curiosity.

Another anchor: give yourself permission to be picky. You aren't auditioning for a corporate job with a long list of prerequisites; you're curating a circle that honors who you are now. It's okay to prefer companions who share your pace, your curiosity, and your taste for a good snack. It's okay to say you're not up for a weekly dinner rotation because you want to protect quiet Sundays for yourself. The great irony of older friendship is that when you stop chasing every potential friend, you start attracting people who truly fit. And when you find a couple of people you genuinely click with, you'll realize that the transfer-student fear was mostly about the awkward moment before a new connection becomes a real one.

Giving new friendships time to settle is the most honest investment you can make.

You don't need to sprint through the onboarding process; you need to show up consistently, be yourself, and trust that the right people will meet you there. You'll get better at recognizing red flags without turning every warning light into a full-blown crisis. And if you're ever tempted to act as though you're auditioning for a role in a soap opera—the one where everyone is drama and no one is human—remember this: your best friend is the one who treats you like a person with a life, not a plot device in someone else's story.

THE HIGH-MAINTENANCE FRIEND VS. THE HIGH-VALUE FRIEND

If you've spent time with women who have mastered both grace and a little sass, you know the difference between a high-maintenance friend and a high-value friend is not about money or status; it's about energy exchange. A high-maintenance friend feels like a full-time job you didn't apply for. She needs constant rescuing—emergencies that require your mental real estate, your calendar, and your patience to stay in a perpetual hold pattern. She often expects you to adjust your life around her needs, leaving you with a sense of being walked through a relay race that never ends. You might love her fiercely, but you notice you're shrinking to fit her expectations, and that shrinking isn't optional; it's exhausting. A high-value friend, by contrast, fills your cup. She shows up in your life with a mix of generosity, honesty, and healthy boundaries. She celebrates your wins, helps you reflect on your mistakes with kindness, and leaves more energy in your day than she takes away. She also tells you the truth—even when it's a little uncomfortable—because she trusts the relationship enough to hold space for both your growth and hers.

The practical question is this: what does a healthy exchange look like in real life? It's not a performance; it's a pattern you can notice and nurture. Does your friend ask about your week, not just your latest crisis? Do you feel supported during big moments and mundane ones alike? When you need reassurance, does she offer a thoughtful, honest response rather than a hurry-up compliment or a generic pep talk? On the other side, do you offer the same in return—time, listening, energy, and a willingness to say no to protect the relationship from tipping into resentment? High-value doesn't mean perfect; it means sustainable. It's the difference between a long, steady climb and a roller coaster that ends in a dizzy heap.

Sometimes the test comes in small, almost comic moments. If a friend consistently makes plans that leave you with the consequences of a hangover you didn't sign up for—late-night texts, last-minute gatherings, or constant last-minute favors—you're not obligated to keep bending your schedule to accommodate that pattern. You can lean into a conversation that feels like a check-in rather than an accusation. A simple, "I value our friendship, and I want to protect it. I can't always be available on that timeline. Can we plan with a bit more notice?" can be the difference between a brittle dynamic and a sturdy, nourishing one. You deserve that steadiness.

The aim here isn't to turn every friend into a mirror of your own needs or to keep people who drain you around out of habit. It's to align your circle with your current season: people who will cheer for you when you take a risk, who tolerate your quirks without punishing you for them, and who will be honest with you even when the truth is awkward. If you can identify those qualities and set your own boundaries with warmth and clarity, you'll know you've found a rhythm that lets you be your best self without turning your life into a constant negotiation.

What you're really cultivating is a circle that doesn't pretend to be perfect. It's a circle that's honest about its limits, generous where it can be, and playful where it should be. In the end, this isn't about accumulating friends; it's about creating a village that makes aging less lonely and a lot more deliciously loud. And if you ever worry that you're turning into a boundary-obsessed person, remember: boundaries are the soil that lets your friendships grow—strong, resilient, and rightly yours.

CONFLICT, REPAIR, AND HONEST CONVERSATIONS

Conflict isn't the enemy of friendship; it's the pressure valve that prevents steam burns and resentment from piling up into one dramatic boiler explosion. The trick is not avoiding friction but handling it with the kind of clarity you wish your old glasses would offer you—steady, a little forgiving, and somehow more comfortable once you've adjusted them. The simplest truth is this: conversations that matter deserve to be direct, kind, and specific. You don't want to win the argument; you want to preserve the relationship while addressing what's actually bothering you.

A basic framework helps. Start with a neutral opening that names the moment without accusing the other person. For example, you could say, *I've been feeling a bit overwhelmed by our last few plans, and I want to figure out how we can both feel good about them.* Then share the impact with I-statements that focus on your experience rather than their character. You might say, *I feel stretched thin when plans change at the last minute because I rely on routine to manage my energy.* Pauses matter here. Give the other person time to hear you, to process, and to respond. The goal is not to drop a clutch of grievances but to reset a pattern that works for both of you.

Here are a few real-world exchanges that land with practical honesty. The first is a gentle invitation to clarity: "I care about our friendship, and I want to keep supporting each other. Could we talk about how often we check in and how we handle last-minute invites? It would help me feel less overwhelmed." The second is a boundary that protects your time without erasing affection: "I love when we're together, but Sundays are sacred for rest. If we could keep Sundays free for a long walk or a book, I'd be grateful." The third is about repair after a misstep: "When you forgot to call last week, I felt unimportant. I'm not blaming you; I'm telling you how it landed on me, and I'd love to hear what was going on for you." These are not scripts to memorize; they're templates to adapt to your voice.

Boundaries aren't punishments; they're invitations to trust. When you name a boundary with warmth and a touch of humor, you give the other person something real to respond to instead of a vague feeling of irritation. Humor is a powerful ally here. A light remark—like, "Let's treat our calendar like a sacred museum: no last-minute chaos tours"—can defuse tension and remind both of you that you're in this together. The goal is not to score points but to understand, repair, and move forward with fresh clarity.

If a conflict surfaces repeatedly with the same person and you find yourself doing the emotional wrangling more than the other party, step back. You're allowed to pause and reassess whether this relationship should continue in its current form. You're not a failure for choosing energy over drama; you're a strategist protecting your life force. The most mature move is often a conversation that begins with truth, continues with listening, and ends with a plan. And yes, you can still laugh together afterward—the best repairs usually come with a wink and a shared memory that reminds you both of why you're in this friendship in the first place.

YOUR SOCIAL LIFE NEEDS RECOVERY TIME

If your social life feels like a high-speed chase through a maze of group chats, calendars, and event flyers, you're not alone. The truth about friendships after sixty is not that you must vanish into a quiet house with a cat on your lap;

it's that your energy has a budget, and you get to decide how to spend it. Your social life needs recovery time the way a garden needs rain. You don't plan every watering day around the clock; you let the soil breathe, you rest, and you show up when you have something to offer that's truly you. Recovery time is not laziness; it's strategic investment in your emotional and physical well-being. It's how you keep your enthusiasm intact for the long haul, not just the next month.

Recovery time can look like small but mighty rituals. A couple of quiet days between heavy social events can prevent the dreaded social burnout—the kind that makes you retreat into a pillow fort rather than a party. When you schedule your calendar, you don't just block out events; you block out the space between events. You reserve time for rest, reading, a long walk, or a series you're bingeing because you deserve a slow-down that isn't framed as laziness or guilt. This isn't selfish; it's sustainable. A rested you shows up as a better friend, a more present listener, and a person who can bring something real to a conversation rather than a tired anecdote and a sigh.

Energy budgeting extends beyond personal time. It means choosing how you engage with social media, how you handle invitations, and how you respond to pervasive, urgent requests. You don't owe the world a constant stream of availability. The right boundary here is a respectful but firm boundary: respond on your terms, with your schedule in mind. A simple message—*I can do Thursday evening and Saturday afternoon next week. Which works better for you?*—gives you control without burning the bridge. And if you're offered a chance to join a social event that doesn't excite you, you're allowed to say no. You can acknowledge the invitation with grace and offer a future option that feels more compelling.

A final thought: your social circle isn't something that happens to you; it's something you actively curate. It's not about having a hundred "friends" who never know your real name and dinner schedule; it's about surrounding yourself with a few people who bring joy, accountability, laughter, and a sense that you're seen and understood. You're allowed to rotate out acquaintances for deeper connections, and you're allowed to invite new energy in at a pace that respects your pace.

The reward for this patient cultivation is not merely a fuller calendar; it's a life that feels chosen, inclusive, and deliciously bright—complete with the kind of friendships that make aging feel like a privilege rather than a chore. And when you look around your circle and realize it reflects the life you want to live, you'll know you've earned a new kind of confidence—the confidence to be choosy, to be brave, and to keep choosing you.

SEVEN
FAMILY DYNAMICS, GRANDKIDS, AND THE BOUNDARY OLYMPICS

THE FAMILY GROUP TEXT SURVIVAL PROTOCOL

If your family group chat were a televised drama, it would open with a dramatic notification ping and end with someone accidentally liking their own message and ending the episode in chaos. Welcome to the Family Group Text Survival Protocol, a lighthearted toolkit for participating without surrendering your sense of humor or your sleep schedule. The truth is, group texts can feel like a game of whack-a-mile-long-thread, where every new message escalates from a casual update to a full-blown family meeting at 2 a.m. with emoji yelling and thread-jumping opinions. The good news is you don't have to live inside that buzzing box to stay informed, connected, and somehow sane. You can negotiate the chaos with boundaries that feel natural, not robotic, and still keep your love at the center of the noise.

Start with a simple self-guardrail: decide what counts as essential information and what can be saved for later. When you log in, you scan for the urgent stuff first—the school announcements, a medical update, travel plans, and the cousin's new plant collection that somehow became a family emergency. Then you give yourself permission to skip everything that isn't essential. It sounds almost rebellious to set limits, but it's really about protecting your quiet moments, the ones where you brew tea and pretend the world isn't loudly rearranging itself around you. If someone blurts out a dramatic update about the family reunion in the same breath as a recipe request, you can let the drama breathe without becoming the fire extinguisher. A little distance often reveals what truly needs your attention and what can wait for a calmer hour.

One practical habit is to designate a message-velocity agreement, a gentle rhythm for when replies are expected and when not. You can answer the important messages and tuck the rest away to revisit later. If it helps, set a private reminder in your phone to check the chat at a time that doesn't interrupt a nap or a favorite show. The key here is consistency rather than perfection. Family members will test boundaries; a steady, kind response teaches them what is and isn't acceptable without turning you into the villain of the group chat saga. You can respond with warmth and clarity in a way that preserves your energy and preserves relationships.

Another component is a few go-to phrases that keep conversations moving without inviting a novel-length reply from you. You might keep in your back pocket a few lines like: I'm not available to weigh in on this today, but I'll let you know when I am; I appreciate the update and I'll check in later; I can help coordinate within a limited window, but I can't be on-call 24/7; I'll add this to my notes and we can revisit after breakfast. These phrases feel small, almost ceremonial, but they carry weight. They say you care, you're present, and you have boundaries that matter. The beauty is in the repetition: over time, people learn the rhythm and you save your energy for the moments that truly deserve it.

Humor is the secret seasoning that makes boundaries palatable. When a thread spirals into a barrage of memes and unsolicited life hacks, you can reply with a lighthearted nudge: I came for the cute dog video, not the family council meeting. If someone tries to draft you into planning eternity with a single emoji, you can respond with a wink and a practical solution: let's pick a date, I'll bring the potato salad, you bring the calendar. Humor helps you stay human and keeps the tone from tipping into sharp corners. It also models resilience for younger family members who watch how you handle the noise and still show up with love.

The protocol isn't about retreat; it's about boundaries that feel safe and sustainable. It's about carving out space for your own life within a network that loves you and often forgets you're a real person with a person's needs. It's about learning when to leap into the conversation, when to nod politely from the balcony, and when to hand the thread off to someone else who thrives on all the drama. And because life with family is a long-running series, you're not choosing a one-episode fix. You're drafting a season-long approach that keeps you present without becoming overwhelmed. As you apply these habits, you'll notice the group thread relaxes its grip on your mornings, you regain the quiet that fuels your best days, and you still feel connected to the people who matter most. That balance is not only possible; it's deliciously within reach.

The next step is to test your protocol during a typical week: watch for a handful of essential updates, respond with one of your go-to phrases, and schedule a check-in in a calmer hour. You'll likely discover that the group chat doesn't demand your every breath; it only requires your presence at the right times. And when you do show up, you'll be there with a steadier voice, a lighter spirit, and a clearly remembered purpose: to love the family and protect your own peace at the same time. So take a breath, set your boundaries, and step into the chat with the confidence that you can participate joyfully—

without losing the thread of your own life in the process.

GRANDMOTHERING YOUR WAY

Grandmothering is less about a single script and more about a living anthology of your style. Some days you're the hands-on storyteller who chews bubble gum and narrates backyard adventures with your grandkids. Other days you're the quiet, reliable anchor who shows up with cookies and a listening ear and lets the kids' laughter teach you the language of this new generation. Either way, you bring a voice that matters, a boundary that protects your energy, and a sense of humor that makes any family moment a little lighter. The trick isn't to fit into a mold; it's to wear your own shape with pride, knowing that your presence, in whatever form, is the gift your family receives.

Think about the stamp you want to leave on grandmotherhood. Are you the grandma who knows every school play by heart, who irons tiny costumes and sneaks a scarf of glitter into the finale? Or are you the grandma who cherishes the quiet moments, who sneaks in a snack, a story, and a steady presence, and then steps back to let the children make their own messes and memories? Either approach is valid, and both benefit from boundaries that are as gentle as they are firm. The key is to align your actions with your energy, not with your sense of obligation. You don't owe your family a tour of your calendar every Sunday just because you exist. You owe them your love, your presence when you can offer it, and your respect for your own life.

When you're deeply involved, your days can feel like a mosaic of carpool lines, school concerts, and approved snacks for every little event. You may volunteer for the bake sale because your grandson's smile melts your heart, and then discover that you've also signed up for color-coding the entire event, making phone calls, and orchestrating a mini fund-raiser. That is a sweet problem to have, but it's still a problem if it steals your own rest. In those moments, you step back and remember the core of grandmothering: presence, not pressure. If your style is "joyfully not on-call," you can still be a warm lighthouse in the fog—frequent enough to be relied upon, scarce enough to protect your own evenings and Sunday afternoons.

A practical approach is to draft your own grandmothering playbook, a flexible guide you carry with you into every family interaction. It might include a few lines you've practiced for boundary setting, a couple of activities you enjoy sharing with your grandkids, and a handful of non-negotiables that keep you from being stretched too thin. You might decide that you'll attend one school event per season if that's your limit, or that you'll host one special family ritual that belongs to you—like a summer tea party with all your favorite stories and a playlist of songs that make everyone smile. This is not about shrinking your role; it's about shaping it so that your presence is something your family looks forward to, rather than something that exhausts you.

The most generous gift you can offer your family is a version of you that remains authentic and joyful. When you model healthy boundaries, you teach the next generation how to hold their own lives with respect for the people around them. And you show the grandchildren that aging isn't a surrender; it's a declaration of wisdom, a treasure trove of stories, and a reservoir of reliability they can count on. As you navigate grandmothering your way, you'll find that your children—now adults with families of their own—appreciate a grandmother who is present without becoming overwhelmed. You'll discover you can be both kind and clear, generous with your heart and protective of your time. The family dynamic shifts in your favor not because you demand it, but because you model a sustainable, loving rhythm they want to emulate.

Grandmothering is a dialogue, not a monologue. It's a practice of showing up for the moments that matter and choosing yourself for the moments that don't. It's about letting your love be the center of the room while your boundaries keep the room from spinning out of control. And as you embrace your own style, you'll notice an unexpected side effect: your grandchildren, your children, and your siblings will respond to your clarity with greater ease and affection. The family you're shaping—with humor, care, and steadiness—becomes the family you want to be part of when you look back on these years.

In the next part, we'll talk about saying no without writing a novel. Because sometimes the most powerful thing you can offer your family is a concise, compassionate boundary that keeps everyone moving forward with dignity and love.

SAYING NO WITHOUT WRITING A NOVEL

Boundaries deserve to be short, sweet, and unsentimental when the moment calls for them. If saying no feels like a tug-of-war between your desires and someone else's expectations, you're not alone. The trick is to deliver your limits with warmth and clarity, like a well-timed compliment that also delivers a necessary instruction. People respond to boundaries when they're paired with kindness and a touch of humor rather than guilt and lectures. You have earned the right to guard your time, your energy, and your peace, and you get to do it without overexplanation or long-winded apologies. The boundary is not a wall; it's a doorway you're choosing to keep open for the life you want to live.

The simplest way to begin is with brief, direct phrases that leave little room for debate or negotiation. You can practice lines that fit many situations: I can't take this on right now, but I can help with a plan next week. I'm not available for that event, but I'd love to catch up by phone soon. I'm sure you understand, but I need to protect my sleep and my health, so I'll pass on this one. Short sentences, warm tone, clear outcomes. The more you use them, the more natural they feel. You're not shirking responsibility; you're prioritizing well-being. And that, in itself, is a form of care.

Another useful tactic is to redirect with an alternative that keeps the connection alive while setting a boundary. If a relative asks you to host a large gathering every holiday, you might respond with a grateful acknowledgment and offer a smaller, more manageable plan: I'd love to celebrate with you, but a big event isn't feasible this year. What if we do a potluck brunch at my place and a quick video call for the cousins who live far away? The secret is to keep the energy high and the expectations realistic. You're not saying no to family; you're saying yes to a version of family life that works for you.

When it comes to health and medical decisions, boundaries are especially crucial. You can be supportive and still advocate for your own limits. A typical boundary in this arena might be: I've got the chart you asked me to review, and I'll make notes this afternoon. I won't be making decisions on the spot, but I'll respond after I've reflected. Or: I respect your need to know everything, but I'm not comfortable discussing every detail here. Let's schedule a time where we can talk without a crowd and with a clear agenda. These sentences aren't stone; they're negotiation tools that preserve your dignity and protect your time.

A few practical reminders: write down two or three phrases you're comfortable using in different scenarios, rehearse them in front of a mirror or during a quick walk, and keep them accessible on your phone. Apply these lines consistently, even when you feel a twinge of guilt or fear of disappointing someone. Boundaries are not about winning or losing; they're about creating a structure that allows you to show up as your best self in every relationship. In time, these phrases become automatic, like muscle memory for kindness that also preserves your health and your joy.

As you practice, you'll notice something

important: people will adjust their expectations, not because they've been masterfully defeated by your resolve, but because they've learned how you operate. You'll be met with more cooperation, less resistance, and a greater sense that your family's needs and your needs can exist in the same room. And when you slip, as we all do, you'll slip with grace, not guilt, and you'll try again with the same grace. The point isn't perfection; it's sustainability—the kind that makes your days kinder, calmer, and more you. The next section will explore how this plays out during the holidays, when traditions collide with travel and drama, and when you're trying to keep the peace without becoming the peacekeeper who never sleeps.

HOLIDAYS: MANAGING TRADITIONS, TRAVEL, AND DRAMA

Holidays should feel like warm blankets and favorite songs, not obstacle courses. Yet for many of us, the season arrives with a swarm of relatives, a mile-long set of traditions, and the kind of drama that makes the Grinch feel like a civics teacher. The good news is that you can reclaim the joy with a few practical shifts that lighten the load without dampening the spirit. The first move is permission—to simplify. Traditions are meaningful because they make us feel connected, not because they demand a marathon of obligations. You get to choose which rituals you carry forward and which ones you adapt or retire. A simple rule helps: if it doesn't nourish you or the people you love, you can reimagine it. A single, well-loved tradition can carry the holiday season with quiet dignity better than a dozen obligations that exhaust you.

Travel is a frequent source of stress, especially when the itinerary feels like a military operation. The trick is fewer moving parts, not fewer memories. Consider consolidating travel into one central day, booking in a way that honors your energy levels, and building buffers for rest and recoup time. You can plan less driving and more stopping, more snacks, more chance to catch your breath. If you're the family navigator, you might rotate responsibility so the same person isn't carrying the mental map every year. If you're not driving, you can offer visions of the trip's atmosphere:

a playlist, a photo album you'll create later, a shared journal of moments. Small, thoughtful offerings provide a sense of participation without shattering your routines.

Drama loves a stage, especially around the holidays. Boundaries are the backstage crew that keeps the show running smoothly. You can designate a Drama-Free Zone for certain conversations and times, a quiet corner of the house or a specific window into the day when you agree to pause the emotional fireworks. You can also schedule a "holiday reset" moment when everyone drops their burdens for a current celebration and then returns to them with refreshed energy. The hallmark of a sane holiday is not perfection but a workable pace that respects your health, your sleep, and your sanity. You can tell the family the plan with warmth: we're keeping things simple this year to maximize the joy we feel when we're together, and we'll each contribute what we can, without the pressure to be perfect.

The most important ingredient of holiday harmony is your own legacy of calm. When you model a gentler pace, you teach your family that joy does not require a heavy toll. You show your grandchildren that celebrations can be meaningful without becoming exhausting. You demonstrate to your siblings and adult children that love can exist alongside boundaries that keep everyone healthy. Your choices ripple outward, creating a family culture in which the holidays are a feast of connection rather than a battlefield of expectations. And as you lead with intention, you'll find the season sparkling with a quiet brilliance that no glitter can match. In the next section we'll turn to a different kind of gravity—the moment you become the family anchor, and how to protect your own life while still showing up with love.

WHEN YOU BECOME THE "FAMILY ANCHOR"

Some days you wake up and realize you're not just the grandma in the kitchen; you're the quiet gravity that keeps the whole orbit from spinning away. Becoming the family anchor means you're the person others count on for steadiness, not necessarily the person who does everything for everyone. It's a role that can feel both comforting and heavy, like carrying a treasured, fragile lamp that lights the room without burning your hands. The trick is to embrace the responsibility with a clear sense of your own boundaries and a plan for your life that remains intact while you hold space for others.

First, protect your time like a precious resource. If your calendar resembles a calendar sculpture with edges that bleed into every other week, you're not alone, and you're not doomed. You can create blocks for yourself that are nonnegotiable, even if it's just a single hour on a Tuesday for a walk, a coffee, or a chapter in your current book. Let family know that your time is limited but real, and offer a reliable alternative. You might say, I can meet on Tuesdays after 4, but not before. I'll be glad to help coordinate meals this week, but I can't take on five extra errands this Saturday. You'll find that your counter offers become a lifeline for others who rely on your steady presence while granting you the freedom to live your life outside your role as anchor.

Boundaries with love are especially vital when you're juggling caregiving obligations. It's wonderful to be there for a parent who needs assistance, but you're not a full-time caregiver unless you choose it. If you're called on to be the central caregiver, you can acknowledge the request with gratitude and propose a sustainable plan. The phrase I appreciate the trust you've placed in me, and I can do X hours a week with Y support from Z, may be the most hopeful sentence you'll ever say in this context. It's specific, it's actionable, and it protects your own energy while honoring the needs of your loved ones. You deserve to live outside the role of "the one who never says no." The moment you call out your limits clearly, you invite others to step in and share the load, which is how healthy families grow.

Being the anchor also means you have a responsibility to model a life you want to live. It's not a badge you wear to prove your indispensability; it's a reminder that you are part of the family's foundation and that your best self is a gift others benefit from. This might mean maintaining a couple of non-negotiables for your own wellness—regular doctor visits, enough sleep, time to pursue a hobby that keeps your brain young and your heart full. If your family sees you investing in your own vitality, they begin to understand that your love for them is not dependent on your exhaustion. You become a living example of resilience, grace, and humor alike.

Sometimes becoming an anchor means letting go of the urge to fix every problem before breakfast. You can be the guiding voice without being the one who solves every argument or takes on every crisis. You offer clarity, you set boundaries, and you step away when your energy runs low, knowing that love is more sustainable when it's honest. Your presence is not a compromise; it's a choice you make every day to show up as your genuine self. And when you do, you'll find your family —young and old—richer for the steadiness you bring, more confident in their own hearts, and deeply grateful for the quiet, unglamorous strength that has become your signature.

The boundaries you set and the life you protect aren't selfish; they're essential. They create space for the people you love to grow in healthier ways and for you to remain a person who can keep showing up—joyful, stubborn, playful, and true. As you navigate this chapter of family life, remember that you can be both anchor and traveler, ballast and buoy. The balance isn't a straight line; it's a gentle arc that you draw with intention, humor, and a confidence that age has earned you. You are exactly the kind of wisdom and warmth the people who matter most need, and you deserve to keep writing your own story even as you hold them close. This is your time to shine with boundary-made brightness, and to keep loving your people with a lightness that never sacrifices your own life.

EIGHT
DATING, COMPANIONSHIP, AND "DO I EVEN WANT THIS?"

THE DESIRE SPECTRUM

What do you want from companionship at this stage, and when did that become either a punchline or a passport stamp you're proud to flash? The truth is simple and delicious: desire at sixty isn't a single shade of gray. It's a spectrum, full of surprising colors, surprising comfort levels, and surprising honesty you've earned the right to claim. Some days you want a partner who feels like a warm mug of tea after a long day. Other days you want a travel buddy who isn't allergic to last minute road trips and questionable hotel breakfasts. And some days you wake up and realize what you really want is a fabulous lack of drama—someone who doesn't require your whole life to be a audition tape for a romance novel. Naming these wants isn't capitulation; it's strategy, and it's perfectly okay to redraw the map as you go.

The first step is giving yourself permission to have preferences that don't have to fit into a neat, tidy box. The desire spectrum includes companionship, friendship, romance, casual connection, steady companionship with no romance at all, someone who loves your grandchildren as much as you do, or someone who understands that your independence is non negotiable. It can include the thrill of a spark or the comfort of a familiar, steady presence. It can include a pause button on dating altogether, followed by a different kind of curiosity later on. The point is not to choose a single path and pretend it's your destiny; it's to name what would make your days feel more aligned with who you are now, in this moment.

Let's try a quick exercise in naming. If you could wave a magic wand and guarantee one ordinary thing in your week—no dramatic plot twists, just a reliable thread—what would it look like? Would you enjoy evenings with someone who shares your love of a quiet glass of wine and the same brand of ridiculous TikTok videos, or would you prefer weekends that feel like spontaneous mini adventures with someone who says yes to a last-minute road trip even when you're packed for a staycation? Do you crave conversation that rumbles on long after the television goes quiet, or do you prefer comfortable silences that don't demand a single emotional monologue?

Desire isn't a trap; it's a compass. Your compass can happily point toward "absolutely yes," toward "maybe," or toward "absolutely not," and that final direction does not declare you a bad person or a commitment-phobe. It simply marks your boundaries and your boundaries alone. The more you name your preferences honestly, the more you'll attract people who don't waste your time or your energy with mismatched expectations. And yes, that means occasionally saying no, even to something with potential, because your yes matters.

What you want in the intimate or relational sphere matters because it colors every interaction you have from here on out. It shapes how you present yourself online, how you show up for a first date, and how you decide when a connection isn't worth the effort. It also helps you avoid the exhausting cycle of trying to fit into someone else's story instead of writing your own. This isn't cynicism; it's clarity, and it's the kind of clarity that grows kinder and funnier the more you practice it.

So, we name the spectrum, own our preferences, and decide how we want to show up in the dating world without apologizing for wanting something that makes life richer—not heavier. In the days ahead, you'll learn how to translate that understanding into online profiles, conversations that feel real, and boundaries that stay strong, even when romance socializes and starts to flirt with your nerves. The path you choose can be playful, respectful, and well within your control. And if you ever forget, some of the best reminders come dressed as a ridiculous dating app notification or a hilariously bad first-impression photo—proof that love and life can still surprise you with a wink.

Let this be your invitation to embrace the nuance, to refuse the false simplicity of a "one size fits all" romance, and to step forward with humor, honesty, and a clear sense of what your heart wants—and doesn't want. The next step is taking that clarity into the real, modern world of online dating, where profiles, messages, and first dates are your new playground.

Bridge to next section: once you've named your desires, you'll want to translate them into a dating profile that feels like you and a conversation approach that respects your boundaries without dulling your sparkle.

ONLINE DATING WITHOUT LOSING YOUR MIND

Online dating can feel like sprinting a marathon in a pair of brand-new slippers: awkward, risky, and somehow you're still hopeful about a better future. If your knee joints crack in protest at the thought of swiping, you're not alone. If you're excited by the possibility of meeting someone who actually gets your jokes and respects your independence, you're in good company. The goal here isn't speed. It's alignment: a profile that tells the truth, a set of messages that stays light but honest, and a pace that honors your energy levels.

Start with the profile—your personal billboard that says, in a single glance, who you are and what you're looking for. You don't have to pretend you're a younger version of yourself to attract a certain type of attention. You just have to be clear, specific, and witty in a way that betrays no fear of being your authentic self. A profile with personality—your voice, your humor, your quirks—will attract people who respond to that energy rather than those who want a polished mask. Include a few specifics that tell someone what life with you looks like: the kind of weekend you love, a harmless pet peeve (like people who pronounce "sushi" like it's a fashion trend), and the small rituals that make your days brighter.

When it comes to messaging, think of it as a conversation you'd actually like to have, not a performance you're auditioning for. Be direct but kind. Lead with a question or a light observation that invites a response, not a monologue about your illustrious career or your last gym routine. Avoid the trap of overthinking every word; simply respond with curiosity and warmth. A good opener isn't a set of rehearsed lines; it's a doorway to shared humor or common ground. And if you don't feel a spark, give yourself permission to move on without apology. The goal is not to collect stories of romance gone wrong but to land a real connection that respects your needs and your energy.

Profile do's and don'ts aren't about policing your life; they're about protecting your time and dignity. Do be honest about your availability, which can be as important as your interests. Don't pretend you're ready for a late-night call if your energy peaks at 7 p.m. Do share what you're looking for, whether that's companionship with occasional dating moments, a long-term partner, or simply a kind person to enjoy a lazy Sunday with. Do consider safety features your ally: complete privacy settings, the ability to block someone who makes you uncomfortable, and a plan to verify who you're talking to before you share personal information. Don't reveal addresses, work details, or travel plans too quickly. And if a conversation takes a turn for the suspicious—requests for money, pressure to move quickly, or vague promises—trust your instincts and disengage.

Real-world tips for profiles and messaging come with a sense of humor because dating after sixty is ripe for punchlines—and perhaps even better for real connection than you expected. When you present your best self online, you'll notice that the conversations you want to have start to show up in your inbox. You'll also notice a surprising thing: you have the power to decide when something is worth a real conversation and when it's not worth a single thought.

As you refine your bio, you'll also learn to filter for what matters: safety, shared values, and a mutual respect for your independence. And yes, you'll learn to laugh at the mismatches—the same way you laugh at a truly terrible first date story with your friends. The point isn't to become a dating-app master; it's to preserve your dignity while exploring the possibility of companionship. The more you practice, the more fun it becomes, and the more likely you are to encounter someone who makes your life feel a little brighter without draining your battery.

Bridge to next section: once you've built a

profile and learned how to message with your voice, you'll still need to balance enthusiasm with caution. That's where safety comes in—two steps forward in rhythm, not a leap into the unknown.

SAFETY FIRST, SPARK SECOND

Dating after sixty can feel like stepping into a perfect storm of possibility and risk, and the real secret is simple: guard the spark without letting the shadows steal your confidence. Safety isn't a killjoy; it's the quiet, practical friend who shows up early, holds your hand, and then lets you unlock the door to a good time with your own terms. You deserve experiences that feel thrilling, not traumatic, and you deserve to keep your private life, well, private until you're ready to share it. This section serves as your playbook for keeping first contacts light, conversations honest, and meetings secure, so you can enjoy the thrill of connection without paying the price of carelessness.

First, set your boundaries as if you were choosing seats at a restaurant. You want the aisle seat? Fine. You prefer the booth? Also fine. It's your table, your time, and your comfort that matters. In dating terms, that means choosing when to meet, where to meet, and how long you'll stay in the first encounter. Public spaces are not just safer; they're kinder to nerves. A coffee meet-up, a stroll through a busy market, a museum visit, or a charity event offers casual, low-pressure environments that let you observe red flags without feeling trapped by a candlelit illusion. Share your plan with a friend. Text or call a buddy before you leave, during the date if you're comfortable, and after you're back home. It's not paranoia; it's practical care that honors your time and your energy.

Privacy matters as much as punctuality. Don't share your address, your workplace, or your routine with someone you barely know. Use a temporary number or the dating-app messaging system until you've established trust, and keep your personal information under your control. When a conversation starts to veer into intrusive territory, you have every right to exit gracefully. If you're asked for money, favors, or to bend a rule you've set for yourself, you're not being rude—you're being wise. Safety also includes mental and emotional boundaries. If a person's words chip away at your self-esteem, or if their humor veers toward belittling or gaslighting, step back. You deserve respect, not a revolving door of drama.

Another practical precaution is a safety check-in plan. Decide on a friend or family member who will receive a brief update after the date: where you went, who you met, and when you expect to be back. If you don't check in, they'll call someone or come looking. It sounds a little like a spy movie, but so is the moment when you realize you forgot to tell your best friend that you're actually dating again. A quick check-in script can be as simple as: "I'm meeting for coffee with a new person from the app. I'll text you when I'm back." Simple, clear, and effective.

Of course, we want to nurture the spark. That means learning to read the signs of genuine interest versus manipulation. A confident potential partner will respect your boundaries, listen when you speak, and show curiosity about your life rather than pressuring you to adjust it. They'll be patient with your pace, even if your pace includes pausing to check a fact on your own terms. Sparks aren't about quick closings; they're about mutuality. If you feel you're giving more than you're receiving, or you're chasing a trend rather than a connection, step back and reassess. The goal is a relationship that enhances your life, not one that drains it.

Safety isn't a limitation; it's a trampoline you bounce from toward something brighter. With this mindset, you can explore companionship with confidence, knowing that you have the tools to protect your heart and your sense of humor. The next step moves from safety to the delicate conversation about intimacy and body honesty, where truth and comfort walk hand in hand with your laughter and your boundaries.

Bridge to next section: safety sets the stage, but real connection requires a clear, honest conversation about intimacy and how your body feels in this new chapter.

INTIMACY, CONFIDENCE, AND REAL BODIES

Intimacy in later life isn't about chasing a younger silhouette or replaying a past script;

it's about discovering what feels genuine, comfortable, and exciting for you right now. The body you have is a remarkable instrument with a few new quirks—like a car that used to purr and now occasionally coughs out a polite blue flame whenever the weather shifts. Menopause may have left a few cameos, but it didn't erase your capacity for warmth, humor, and desire. In this space we replace shame with curiosity, fatigue with tenderness, and stereotype with experience. You deserve to approach intimacy with the same level of confidence you bring to a long-held friendship: honest, a little playful, and unafraid to set boundaries you can live with.

Let's begin with comfort and consent, two pillars that never go out of style. If you're comfortable exploring intimacy again, you'll want a conversation that's as clear as a whiteboard: what you want, what you don't, and what pace feels right. This is not about performing; it's about connection. You have the right to say yes or no to any level of closeness at any time, and you also have the right to change your mind. The person you're with should honor that. If you're unsure where your energy sits, it's okay to take things slowly.

A slow approach isn't a sign of fear; it's a sign of respect for your evolving body and your emotional readiness.

Menopause can bring changes that feel inconvenient or intimidating, from dryness to sleep disruption to shifts in libido. The practical answer is not to pretend these changes don't exist but to experiment with comfort strategies that work for you. Lubricants and moisturizers aren't a failure of romance; they're smart tools that say you deserve ease. Communication becomes your most powerful instrument: share what feels good, what doesn't, and what could be different. Humor helps here too. A well-timed quip can ease vulnerability and open space for honest dialogue. For example, you might say with a smile, "Let's try something that doesn't involve turning on the ceiling fan as a mood lighting device." Laughter softens nerves and makes room for truth.

Real bodies deserve real talk. Your body has carried you through decades of changes, roles, and adventures. It's your body, not a project to be fixed. Embrace its signals—whether it's fatigue, a craving for a walk rather than a fancy dinner, or a craving for intimacy that respects your energy level. If you're with someone new, a shared check-in about what feels good, what's comfortable, and what could be adjusted helps build a strong foundation. This isn't about turning back the clock; it's about turning toward a version of intimacy that fits the life you're living today: a life that includes humor, resilience, and a deep sense of self.

Confidence grows where you practice self-kindness and honesty. You can feel sensual, desired, and powerful at sixty, seventy, or beyond—that status isn't a relic from the past; it's a badge you've earned with every choice you've made to keep showing up as you. And if you're not sure you want a romantic partner at all, that's perfectly valid too. The test isn't social pressure; it's your own clarity about what makes you come alive. In any case, your sexual and intimate life can be a source of joy, not a source of stress, and humor will remain your most faithful ally when nerves show up uninvited.

As we wrap this intimate chapter, remember: your body is not a problem to fix but a life-long partner that deserves respect, curiosity, and plenty of laughter. If you decide to pursue a connection, let it be with someone who sees you fully—the fully formed, unapologetic you who can still joke about the absurdities of aging and still choose to smile when the moment feels bright. The next section invites a practical question: what does it take to blend lives without losing yourself in the process? We'll explore boundaries around money, space, and independence, so you can decide what kind of living arrangement—or non-living arrangement—fits your well-being and your desires.

Bridge to next section: after you've named your needs and tested the waters of intimacy, the bigger question looms: how does a life partner fit into a family, a home, and a calendar that already belongs to you? Let's talk about Blending Lives (or Not), and how to do it with clarity and grace.

BLENDING LIVES (OR NOT)

Cozying up with a partner later in life can feel like renovating a favorite room: you want to upgrade without losing what you loved about the space in the first place. The best blends honor your independence as much as your companionship. The issue isn't whether you want to share more—it's how you want to share and on what terms. The foundation you build matters because it's the framework for the life you'll actually live together, not the life you'll pretend you're living to please someone else. And yes, this can include money, space, routines, and even how you manage two calendars that somehow multiplied while you weren't watching.

Money is not a dirty word when it's approached with honesty. It's about transparency, not deprivation. Start with a simple, respectful talk about finances: what you're comfortable pooling, what you'd rather keep separate, and how you'll handle shared expenses like groceries, utilities, or travel. You don't have to—nor should you—pretend you're merging a dragon's hoard. A practical approach with frequent check-ins can spare you from future 'whose turn is it to pay' debates and keeps your shared life from feeling like a financial cliff jump. Boundaries around space are similar: what does a joint home look like in terms of quiet hours, guest policies, and personal sanctuaries? It's okay to want a personal corner, a separate studio, or a rotation between households. The goal is not to erase your routine but to weave new rituals that respect both lives.

Independence, space, and personal time aren't signals of disloyalty; they're the oxygen of a healthy partnership. You may want to maintain separate living arrangements for a while, or you may want to blend more fully. Either choice is valid if it aligns with your values and energy. This section isn't about fear of commitment; it's about clear communication and practical boundaries that prevent resentments from growing in the corners of your shared life. If your children, grandchildren, or extended family are involved, you'll want to set expectations with them—this is especially true if you're creating new routines that affect family holidays, caregiving roles, or travel plans. You deserve to invite family into your life in a way that honors your new boundaries rather than eroding them.

In the end, blending lives well is a craft of conversation, not coercion. It's about building a home where your stories continue to matter, where your choices are respected, and where you still have a say in the soundtrack of your days. If you're not ready to blend, that's fine—

your life can be rich with companionship that respects your space and your pace. If you are ready to blend, this is your invitation to design a living arrangement that looks and feels like you, with a partner who respects both your history and your future. Either way, you're steering the ship, and your humor keeps the weather light as you chart the course.

Bridge to next steps: whether you choose to blend or keep your independence, celebrate the choice you've made. This chapter has given you tools to assess, decide, and defend your preferences with grace. The rest of the book will continue to support you with laughter, practical hacks, and the unshakable belief that aging is a stage—one you can lead with confidence and a well-timed punchline.

NINE
TECH, SOCIAL MEDIA, AND SCAMS—A FIELD GUIDE FOR THE BRAVE

SMARTPHONE BASICS THAT ACTUALLY MATTER

If your phone were a roommate, it would be the quiet one who still somehow manages to beep at 3 a.m. and insist on updates during your favorite TV show. The truth is smart devices are incredibly useful when they're behaving, and surprisingly cranky when they're not. This chapter starts with the basics that actually make everyday life easier, not the cliff-notes of every feature you'll never need. Think of it as a small, sturdy toolkit you can rely on instead of a garage full of gadgets you only half understand. You don't need to become a tech savant to win at this game; you just need to know the few functions that matter most in real life.

Begin with a streamlined home screen, because chaos on the main page is chaos in your brain. Put the essentials—Messages, Phone, Camera, and a practical time-saver app—on the first page. Your "one-tap life" should resemble a simple habit: when you unlock the phone, you can text your daughter, check the weather, snap a photo of that new recipe, and set a timer for the oven without hunting through menus. Notifications deserve the same respect. Too many alerts from too many apps create a buzzing background chorus that makes you feel like you're living inside a vending machine. A sensible plan is to keep only the apps you actually use daily on the top screen or in the dock, and tuck everything else into folders you rarely touch. When your screen greets you with peace rather than a carnival, you'll notice how much calmer mornings become.

Battery life is another practical battlefield where small adjustments yield big wins. Dim the brightness to a comfortable level, enable a battery saver mode when you're away from home for the day, and resist the urge to let every app chase your attention with background refresh. Do Not Disturb is your best friend when you're reading, napping, or trying to enjoy a movie without the world pinging you for a sale you didn't even want. You can schedule it to quiet down automatically during the hours you're most likely to be relaxed, and you'll feel a surprising sense of control—a rare commodity after sixty.

Learn to use essential safety and accessibility features with a light touch. A simple "Find My" or "Find My Device" setup can turn panic into practical problem-solving: you can locate a misplaced phone or, if needed, remotely lock or erase it to protect personal information. Emergency features are not just for the dramatic moments; they're for everyday slips, like your phone slipping from your purse in the grocery store and dropping into a sea of carts. You'll realize how often you'll reach for these tools when you've made them easy to access.

Smartphone basics also include thinking about what you actually use regularly. The camera is handy, the calendar keeps you on track, and a couple of trusted apps can simplify tasks like grocery delivery, ride-hailing, or a quick price check when you're out listening for a grandkid's recital. Your device becomes not a fickle gadget but a reliable partner that frees up your time and energy for the things you actually care about—like telling a good story at dinner and still having energy for a walk after.

A quick mental reset before you start: if it's not improving your day, it probably doesn't need to be on your home screen. The point is not to hoard tech; it's to curate it. When you treat your phone as a helpful servant—no drama, no beeping at all hours—you reclaim a little of the calm you deserve. And yes, there will be days when you forget a password, miss a notification, or get caught in a new update loop. That's not failure; that's a sign you're alive in a world that still loves to throw new features at you. You'll learn as you go, and you'll laugh about the stumbles later. Ready to take the next step? Let's talk about how to enjoy social media without letting it pull you into its occasional chaos.

SOCIAL MEDIA: WATCHING BABIES GROW UP AND STRANGERS ARGUE

If you've ever watched a family album come alive on a screen, you know social media can feel like a bustling town square—full of warmth, banter, and occasionally a free-for-all brawl between strangers over opinions they'd never voice in person. The beauty is that you can dip in for the moments that matter and step out before the parade degenerates into a shouting match. The challenge is to enjoy the ride without losing your peace or your sense of humor. This section is your compass for navigating the social clutter with grace, wit, and boundaries that actually stick.

Here's the upside: social platforms let you stay connected with grandkids who live far away, celebrate a friend's new grandchild with a flood of photos, and share a quick, cheerful observation about the world that doesn't require planning a formal get-together. It's a modern scrapbook that can be a daily source of joy if you curate it with intention. The downside is real, too. You'll see heated debates that feel endless, memes that cut a little too close to home, and advice from well-meaning strangers that would have been better kept to the kitchen table. The trick is to treat your feed like a party where you're allowed to leave early if the conversation heads toward a chasm of conflict. The time you save will feel like a gift you gave yourself.

A practical approach is to personalize your feed with care. You can unfollow or mute accounts that spark stress, while still following people whose posts make you smile or remind you of someone you love. It's not about censorship; it's about keeping your emotional climate pleasant. If a post drags you into a debate or ruffles your feathers, pause before replying. Put your thumbs down on the keyboard and let the moment pass rather than fueling a back-and-forth you'll regret later. It's perfectly fine to respond with kindness and a touch of humor—sometimes a light comment about the weather or a light-hearted anecdote is all that's needed to defuse tension.

Privacy is another vital piece of the puzzle. Be mindful of what you share and who can see it. A "public" post might show up in the family chat, on a coworker's feed, or in the eyes of someone you've never met. It's worth spending a minute or two here to check your settings and adjust them so you control who sees your updates. You're not hiding; you're choosing who gets to enjoy your positive moments and who doesn't need to know every detail of your day.

Boundaries are where the real magic happens. Create a few simple lines you're willing to say aloud and a few you'll say with a wink. For example, if someone starts a political pile-on in a comments thread, you can respond with a light-hearted, "Let's keep kindness in the kitchen, shall we?" and then step away. If a friend asks you to take sides on a topic you'd rather not weigh in on, offer a gentle pivot: "I'm here to celebrate, listen, and share what makes my heart happy." Humor can soften almost any dispute, and setting the expectation that you don't engage with every online conflict makes your time on social media more enjoyable.

To keep things buoyant, try a weekly ritual: a 20-minute scroll when you're relaxed, a mental note of the moments that made you smile, and a deliberate step away when the news cycle grows heavy. Remember that social media exists to connect, not to exhaust.

It's a tool, not a verdict on your worth as a person. If you treat it as a curated gallery rather than a news ticker, you'll find yourself laughing more and arguing less. Curious how to use it without losing your cool? Try this approach: follow people who inspire you, block or mute what drains you, and always end each session with a reminder that you can choose to put the device down and live your life in three dimensions—the real one, with a face, a voice, and a conversation that doesn't end with an emoji.

PASSWORDS, FACE ID, AND THE MYTH OF "I'LL REMEMBER"

If your brain were a browser, it would have a dozen tabs open at once, each tab with a warning that you're about to forget something important. It's not your fault—your memory is magnificent in moments, but human beings were never meant to keep track of dozens of unique passwords, codes, and reset links. The reality is you don't need to remember every password and you don't want to reuse the same password across critical accounts. The old habit of using the same word for every website is how you end up with not just one compromised account but several. The good news is there's a simple, safe system that lets you sleep at night without feeling like you're juggling torches.

Begin with the idea of a trusted password manager. A manager is not a betrayal of your memory; it's a friendly vault that stores long, unique passwords and fills them in for you when you need them. The key is to have a strong master password—one that is memorable to you but not something a neighbor could guess. Your master password becomes the key to a small, digital safe that holds all the other keys. Once you've chosen a manager, you'll find that you can generate highly random passwords for each site without ever having to memorize them. You'll also have the option to save login details so you don't fumble through tiny keyboards in a hurry when you're trying to do something simple like paying a bill or logging into your email.

Two-factor authentication is the human equivalent of a second door lock: it makes your accounts much harder to break into. Wherever possible, turn on 2FA. It's not optional because it's a nice extra; it's a shield. It can be as simple as receiving a text code or using an authenticator app, which is a small, inconspicuous step that buys you a lot of peace of mind. Backups matter too. Keep a set of backup codes in a safe place, and consider printing a copy and storing it in a physical file you update yearly. This practice can save you a frantic moment if your device is lost or reset.

Your phone's biometric features—Face ID or fingerprint unlock—are convenient, but they are not a replacement for a strong passcode. Treat biometrics as a fast path to access, not the sole line of defense. Use a reliable passcode as the primary lock and reserve biometrics for everyday use. It's a gentle reminder that convenience and security can share the same space without squinting at the same wall of alarms every time you log in.

A practical routine helps you stay on top of things without becoming obsessive. On a regular day—perhaps Sunday afternoon—update your password manager with any new logins you've created or changed. If you set up two-factor authentication, take a few minutes to familiarize yourself with the backup codes and how to use the authenticator app. Start with the accounts you use most frequently—email, banking, and social platforms—then extend the system to less-used services. The aim is to build muscle memory that protects you without making you feel like you're running a small, digital obstacle course. In time, you'll realize you're not fighting a tidal wave of codes; you're steering a well-managed ship through calmer waters.

You'll notice a quiet confidence growing as you rely on a simple, robust framework rather than on fickle memory. You'll sleep easier, knowing your data is harder to break into and that you can still find your way through your devices with a calm, curious mind. Curious about how to recognize scams that would exploit weak passwords? That's the next frontier, and it's loaded with memorable, practical tips you can actually use in your daily life.

SCAM SPOTTING: THE GREATEST HITS

If something sounds too good to be true, it probably is. If someone demands urgent action, your best move is to pause, breathe, and check the source. Scammers know exactly which strings to pull: fear, greed, loneliness, or a sense that you're missing out on something seductive and easy. They target the same human tendencies you've learned to navigate in the grocery store aisle—the urge to skip a line, the thrill of a quick win, the fear that you'll miss something important. The greatest hits of scams are persistent because they work. The trick is not to become paranoid; it's to become discerning and calm enough to give yourself a moment to decide.

A common category is the text scam, where you get a message that looks like it's from your bank, a government agency, or a loved one in distress. The telltale signs are direct, urgent language, a link you're asked to click, or a request for sensitive information. A quick test is to not click the link and not call the number in the message. Instead, go to the official channel you already trust—your bank's app, the official website, or the customer service line you know by heart—and verify whether there's actually a reason for concern.

Phishing emails leverage logos and layouts that resemble real brands, sometimes with tiny mistakes that a tired eye can miss. They'll push you toward a deadline, a "secure" link, or a form asking for your login. If you feel a flutter of panic or a spark of excitement about a prize or a windfall, that's a moment to pause. A reputable company will never ask you to log in through a link in an email. Instead, they'll direct you to open a new tab and type the official website address yourself, where you'll know you're safe.

Romance scams and "tech support" scams are the classics that have evolved with new lingo. In romance scams, a charming message quickly escalates to a request for money or sensitive information. In tech support scams, an unknown caller insists your computer is compromised and offers to fix it right away, often asking you to install software or share control of your device. If a caller or sender uses high-pressure language or insists on immediate action, that's a red flag you should treat with a healthy dose of skepticism. Remember, you have the power to say no, to take a breath, and to verify through a trusted path.

So how do you respond without exploding a friendship or a family connection? Start with keeping your cool. If you're unsure, tell the caller you'll contact the company directly using a number you look up yourself. Do not use numbers provided in the message. If you've inadvertently clicked a link or shared details, don't panic—log out from the site, run a security check on your device, and consider changing passwords for the affected accounts. It's better to be cautious and clear than to react out of fear and regret.

A few practical markers to walk away with: look for urgent language, grammar oddities, or requests for money, personal information, or remote access. Trust your instinct—if something rings false, it probably is. Block and report suspicious callers or messages, and don't be afraid to tell a friend or family member that you'll verify before you respond. It's a sign of strength to protect your own privacy and to educate yourself about the latest tricks scammers are using. And because you're a savvy reader of life's punchlines, you'll turn these encounters into a quick-whip story you'll tell at the next book club meeting. Want a quick mental checklist for your next suspicious message? Pause, verify, connect through official channels, and remember: you're the one in charge of your digital safety.

If you want to sharpen your scam-spotting

instincts even further, keep a little "safety ritual" in your back pocket. When you receive an unexpected message, take three steps: stop, breathe, and think about whether you would have trusted this person in real life. If the answer is no, you're not being suspicious—you're being sensible. And if you can't verify the source quickly, give yourself permission to disengage, block, and move on. It's not stingy or unfriendly; it's smart and safe. The more you practice saying no to questionable requests, the easier it becomes to protect yourself and your peace of mind without losing your warm, generous spirit.

Ready for the final piece of the puzzle? How to navigate the digital world with support that doesn't require a long-winded tech tutorial every time. That's the goal of the next section: tech support without begging your kids, a plan you can implement today.

TECH SUPPORT WITHOUT BEGGING YOUR KIDS

If you've ever watched a grandchild calmly fix a missing Wi-Fi password while you fumble with the router's blinking lights, you know there's a calm competence you can cultivate without dialing your child in a state of techno-angst. This section is about building a personal, practical tech-support plan that keeps you independent, informed, and less likely to collapse into a pile of "I forgot how to do that" excuses when a device misbehaves. You deserve to be your own best tech advocate as much as you deserve a good laugh when things go sideways.

First, assemble a small, friendly tech toolkit. A notebook that catalogs your devices, OS versions, and the apps you actually use is more valuable than a shelf full of chargers you never need. Include the basics: device model, operating system version, a few key apps, and the password manager you rely on. Create a mental map of where things live—like a treasure map—with simple labels so you can find your own notes quickly. Consider a laminated one-page cheat sheet you keep near your router or by your computer: a few step-by-step anchors for common tasks, such as how to connect to Wi-Fi, how to print from a phone, or how to reset a password. This is not a cheat for cramming memory; it's a responsible, proactive way to stay in control.

Learning is a journey that doesn't require a prodigy brain. The library, community centers, and local workshops are gold mines for adults who want to learn at their own pace. Look for beginner-friendly classes on smartphone basics, privacy and security, or basic computer literacy. Online platforms also offer accessible lessons that cover the essentials—often at your pace and with patient instructors who understand the

TEN
MONEY, DOWNSIZING, AND THE STUFF THAT SOMEHOW MULTIPLIED

AM I OKAY? MONEY CHECK-IN

If money sparks a tiny panic flare in your chest, you're not alone. The first honest money move after sixty isn't a fancy investment strategy or a month-long detox from impulse purchases; it's a simple, friendly check-in with what's actually happening in your wallet and your life. Picture this: you're sipping tea, the house is quiet enough to hear your own thoughts, and you allow yourself a clear moment to peek at the numbers without judgment. The goal isn't perfection; it's clarity. Clarity is kinder than worry, and it's the secret sauce that makes everything else possible.

The Am I Okay? Money Check-In is a low-stress way to understand your financial picture, one page at a time. Start with your income. Where is it coming from? A pension, Social Security, a part-time gig, maybe rental income from the condo you won't sell at the next market dip. Don't worry about making it glamorous; just write down what shows up month to month. Then turn to expenses, beginning with the essentials: housing, utilities, groceries, medications, insurance, transportation. These are the anchors, the pieces that keep your life standing steady when the rest of the world feels like it's wobbling.

Next comes the big but important shift: differentiating the essential from the optional. Essentials fund the basics: a roof over your head, a seat that doesn't crumble when you sit, a pantry that can keep you nourished without becoming an obstacle course. Optional expenses are the little joys that make the days sweeter—the weekly coffee with a friend, the streaming service you actually watch, the occasional splurge you've earned after a month of good budgeting. The key is not to banish joy; it's to ensure it's a deliberate choice, not a default impulse.

As you write, keep your eye on debt, savings, and future planning. Note any debts you carry into this chapter and whether they are manageable within your current income. Do you have a small emergency fund you can rely on when the car acts like a drama queen or the furnace decides to audition for a winter blockbuster? Do you have a plan for medical costs that aren't fully covered by insurance? What about savings for the things you want to do in retirement—a trip, a new hobby, a little cushion for the days when energy slips and you still want to feel in control?

To make this practical, treat the check-in like a one-page cabinet of truths. If you can answer with a steady yes or no, you're ahead. If you find gray areas, these are your signals to pause and adjust. You might discover you're carrying a small monthly expense that sneaks up on you—a subscription you forgot you signed up for, a gym plan you barely use, a storage locker that's only hosting your regrets. The beauty of the exercise is not guilt; it's a gentle, corrective nudge toward outcomes you actually want.

Let me share a concrete example. Meet Lily, sixty-two and newly retired from a long career in education. Her mornings began with a jolt of anxiety as she counted the same numbers again and again: a pension check, a Social Security deposit, and a handful of unpredictable expenses. In an afternoon, she filled out a one-page snapshot: essential monthly costs, a modest cushion for emergencies, and a capped budget for discretionary splurges. The result wasn't perfection; it was a truth she could live with. She saw room to reduce a couple of outdated subscriptions, adjust her grocery plan to lean on seasonal produce, and redirect a small amount toward a life-enhancing goal—maybe a studio in a sunny corner for painting, or a weekly class she'd ignored for years.

The payoff is not a perfect balance sheet; it's the calm you feel when you know where you stand. When you're confident about your baseline, you stop guessing and start guiding. You realize you don't have to be wealthy to be in control; you need to be clear about what you have and what it will support. That clarity then becomes the foundation for every other choice—spending with intention, letting go of excess, and making room for what matters most.

So today, commit to a one-page Money Check-In that you revisit monthly, or at least quarterly. Make it a routine you actually look forward to. When you greet your finances with curiosity and kindness, you'll feel lighter, not louder, about money. And that lightness creates space for the next step in your financial journey: spending with joy, not regret.

SPENDING WITH JOY, NOT REGRET

What if money could be a source of genuine, unforced joy instead of a constant whisper of guilt? The idea sounds scandalously simple, yet it's a powerful shift: spend so that every dollar earned adds meaning to your days, not just fills a squeaky craving that fades in a week. After sixty, your life has a richer texture —more family memories, more experiences that matter, more ways to enjoy the freedom you've earned. It's time to align your money with that life, in a way that feels expansive, not punitive.

The heart of Spending with Joy, Not Regret is a practical philosophy you can live with. Start by identifying what truly matters to you in this chapter of your life. Maybe it's time with grandkids, a reliable car that handles road trips with grace, or a small but steady system that keeps your home warm and safe. Whatever your values are, use them as the compass for every purchase. When you're tempted by a sale or a gadget you don't need, pause and ask a few questions. Will this make my life easier in a meaningful way? Will I smile when I think about it a year from now, not just tomorrow? Is this purchase aligned with the person I want to be at sixty-two, sixty-five, and beyond?

A practical tool is the joy fund—a small, clearly defined portion of your monthly budget dedicated purely to things that bring you happiness. It could be a massage once a month, a weekend away, a new kitchen gadget that actually gets used, or simple indulgences like a favorite book and a comfortable afternoon with tea. The point isn't to hoard joy in a closet of guilt; it's to ensure joy has a seat at the table every month. If you're not using your joy fund, you can roll the money into a larger goal, like a travel plan or a home improvement project that makes daily life easier. The key is consistency and clarity.

Let's bring it to life with a story. Consider Mona, a former project manager who, after retirement, learned to treat money as a measurement of what makes her days brighter. She used her Am I Okay? Money Check-In to map out how much she had for essential expenses and how much she could safely allocate to joy. She experimented with small rewards: a weekly farmers market trip, a monthly pottery class, and a few guided hikes her calendar had always wanted to host but never scheduled. The result wasn't reckless spending; it was a steady rhythm of small wins that fed her energy and kept her social life lively. She even tracked her happiness against each purchase, a little personal scoreboard that reminded her joy was both legitimate and renewable.

A simple rule can protect you from regret: if a purchase doesn't produce significant, lasting joy, consider delaying it for a month. If after thirty days the memory of that item still brings a spark, you've earned a rational excuse to buy it. If not, you've just saved money without sacrificing the things that make life delicious.

Joy isn't about scarcity or compulsive self-denial; it's about making choices that honor your current self—the woman who deserves to savor every moment, who can still be spontaneous, and who doesn't owe any part of her happiness to credit cards. The next step is to bring the clarity of joy into your home by examining how you spend on the everyday and what that says about your priorities. You'll likely find that a few small shifts create a cascade of less stress and more laughter at the end of the week.

What changes will you make this month to lean into joy rather than regret? Consider the purchase you've been half-wanting and half-worrying about. Sit with it for a moment, write down how it would actually impact your days, and then test it against your joy fund. The answers won't be dramatic; they'll be honest. And honesty, at this stage of life, is one of the most valuable kinds of wealth.

DOWNSIZING WITHOUT EMOTIONAL WHIPLASH

Your living space is a memory museum, a physical archive of everything you ever believed would matter to you. The thought of downsizing can feel like surrender, a surrender you don't want to make, and sometimes a surrender you actually need. The art is not about becoming minimal for minimalism's sake; it's about reclaiming space for the life you want to live now. That means sorting, keeping, donating, archiving, and grieving with humor rather than heaviness. When you approach downsizing as a compassionate project rather than a punitive mission, the emotional whiplash eases and even turns into a few good laughs.

First, set the rhythm. Choose a room or a corner you can tackle in a single session, perhaps with a friend who reminds you of your own stubborn streak in the kindest possible way. Begin with a clear goal: what stays, what goes, and what transforms into a memory project that fits into a single box. The memory box is your ally here. You can tuck away a few photos, a letter, a memento from your favorite era, a keepsake that brings a smile when you stumble upon it later. The rest goes through the triage line—keep, donate, archive. You don't have to decide everything in one go; you can do a little each day and celebrate small wins along the way.

Be gentle with your emotional responses. It's natural to feel a surge of attachment or to worry about someone else's memory of your life. Remind yourself that letting go of objects does not erase your story; it makes it easier to tell it in a way that includes the best chapters without dragging around the footnotes. When an item is truly hard to part with, craft a memory box instead. Photograph or document the story, then release the physical piece with a ritual that feels respectful rather than brutal. You can write a brief note to each item as you place it in the memory box or into the donation bag. The act itself becomes a form of closure, a way to acknowledge the importance of the item without surrendering your space.

For the items that hold practical value rather than sentimental weight, poise a practical test: does this item contribute to the quality of daily life in the next year? If the answer is yes, consider a future role for it in a new home. If the answer is no, thank it for its past and make a plan for where it will live now—whether that is to be passed along to someone who will love it or to a charitable organization that will give it a second life.

A useful way to handle the emotional whiplash is to create your own small ritual around downsizing. Say a gentle goodbye to a chair that has given you support for years, or a bookshelf that once held every important novel you've loved. Compost the end with humor, share a story of the item's best moment, and then move forward with your space cleared. You'll find that lifting the physical load also lightens your mental load, and with your home decluttered, you'll feel more able to welcome new adventures.

Now imagine your home in a simplified, warm version of itself—the room you actually use as your favorite reading nook, the kitchen that invites you to cook again, the closet that makes you feel like you have options rather than a hostage to the past. That is the gift of downsizing done with humor and heart: it frees you to live, not to hoard, and it gives your story new, comfortable chapters to inhabit.

PAPERWORK, DOCUMENTS, AND THE DRAWER OF DOOM

If your file drawer could talk, it would probably sigh and say that it has heard enough of your excuses. Paperwork is not glamorous; it's the stubborn pulse in the middle of adulthood, the thing that keeps you from panicking when life gets loud. The Drawer of Doom has a certain charm in its own way—full of receipts, statements, reminders, and the occasional forgotten passport—yet it thrives on chaos. The good news is that you can tame it with a simple, enduring system that is as forgiving as it is practical. The aim is not perfection but reliability: a system you can respect, use, and actually maintain.

Begin with the basic architecture. Create a small set of digital and physical repositories: a core binder for essential documents and a digital folder for scanned copies. Your binder might include sections for medical information, financial statements, legal documents, and household records. The digital folder should mirror the binder, with clear, consistent naming conventions so you can find anything in a pinch. When naming files, be direct and descriptive: the year, the document type, and a brief subject. This makes sense at a glance and saves you from a future treasure hunt through a sea of confusing filenames. Digital copies don't replace the originals, but they do offer a fast, secure backup that is easy to access when you're traveling, busy, or exhausted.

Security is a companion to order. Store originals in a fireproof safe or a bank safe deposit box for the truly important items: birth certificates, wills, powers of attorney, healthcare proxies, and long-term care directives. For everything else, scan, save, and back up. Then shred what you don't need, with care and a small ceremony for the things that deserve a proper goodbye. The act of shredding is not just physical; it's symbolic—it signals to your future self that you are choosing clarity over clutter and control over chaos.

A practical rhythm keeps the system alive: do a yearly audit, ideally around tax time or on a date that has meaning for you. Go through the essential files, confirm that contact information is up to date, verify beneficiaries, and refresh any outdated documents. If you don't have a trusted person to consult, set up a simple plan for how to share this information with your executor or a chosen confidant. Transparency is a form of care—for you and for the people who care about you.

Within this structure, you'll avoid the Drawer of Doom's gravitational pull. Instead, you'll enjoy the ease of knowing where things live, the confidence that your important data is safe, and the speed with which you can respond to life's twists—whether it's a sudden move, a medical change, or a new opportunity on the horizon. The difference is not only practical; it's peace of mind wearing a sane, accessible format.

As you tidy your documents, you'll realize that organization is not a single act but a habit you establish. When you can locate the information you need in moments, you reclaim time for what you want to do instead of what you have to do. The Drawer of Doom stops bullying your day, and your life keeps moving forward with less friction and more humor.

TALKING MONEY WITH FAMILY

Money conversations with family can feel like negotiating a peace treaty on a crowded holiday table. The tension is real, but so is the possibility for clarity, dignity, and even a little humor. Talking money with family is less about verdicts and more about shared understanding—which means you set a boundary, you state a plan, and you invite collaboration rather than confrontation. The goal is transparency that protects your autonomy while honoring the people who care about you.

Begin with a firm, kind boundary: this is the space where you talk about money openly, but you do not allow currencies of control or guilt to cross the threshold. When the conversation comes up, frame it as a practical discussion about how life will be managed going forward, not a passive list of things owed or owed to you. For example, you might open with a simple note: I want to share what I have, what I can do, and what I can't; then we can decide together how to handle shared expenses, caregiving, and future planning. Clarity reduces drama and sets expectations.

One effective approach is to anchor the conversation in your current reality and your desired future. Outline your income, your fixed expenses, and your non-negotiables for personal independence. Then invite your family to share their needs and concerns, listening with the calm you would offer a friend. If a family member asks for money, respond with a structured script in your own words: I appreciate you, and I want to help in ways that fit my budget and my boundaries. Here are the options I can offer today, and here is what we can revisit if circumstances change. This keeps you in the driver's seat while remaining compassionate.

Another practical tactic is to schedule regular money check-ins. A monthly 20-minute conversation in which you review the budget, discuss upcoming expenses, and adjust as needed creates a predictable rhythm that reduces the fear of the unknown. If someone pushes for immediate changes or special treatment, you have a ready response to preserve both financial health and family harmony: a gentle reminder that steady progress beats sudden, unsustainable generosity, and that your goal is to ensure everyone's needs are met without overextending yourself.

The real reward is not just financial clarity but a strengthened sense of trust. When your family sees that you're serious about your own independence, they're more likely to respect boundaries and contribute ideas, not pressure. You'll still have the warmth of shared meals, the comfort of a connected family, and the freedom to say yes to the things that light you up. And the best part is that you can carry these conversations forward into future chapters of life with the same tone: honest, practical, and steadfastly kind.

ELEVEN
CONFIDENCE, STYLE, AND LIVING LOUDLY (EVEN IF YOUR KNEES OBJECT)

THE CONFIDENCE MYTH: IT'S NOT A MOOD, IT'S A PRACTICE

Confidence is not a mood you wake up in and hope to stumble into like a stray cat you name in your sleep. It's a practice you build with small, repeatable actions, especially on mornings when you feel more like a cranked-up kettle than a person ready to take on the world. Think of confidence as a muscle, one you've had since you learned to ride a bike, one that gradually strengthens not because you woke genius-brilliant, but because you kept showing up for practice even when you muttered under your breath that you'd rather skip the set and binge a show instead. And here's the secret you'll come back to again and again: confidence isn't about pretending your knees aren't complaining or your complexion miraculously clearing up; it's about choosing to exist as you, on purpose, with a plan and a little bit of attitude you've earned through decades of living through small, imperfect moments. You're not chasing a spark; you're laying down a rhythm.

Your decades of experience are not evidence of weakness but proof that you've already navigated fear while still making the next call, finishing the project, or showing up at the dinner table with a story that matters. You've negotiated family dynamics, weathered doctors' visits, and kept a sense of humor through the long list of things that change after sixty. Confidence grows when you break big leaps into bite-sized actions. Start with something that won't topple your calendar stone by stone but will nudge you toward the life you want. Acknowledge the fear, then pick a tiny dare: greet the new neighbor with more warmth than caution; propose a plan to your doctor that you'll keep a simple symptom log; or simply forward a message to a friend inviting them to split a morning walk. The point is not to prove you're fearless; it's to demonstrate that you're in charge of the sentence your day writes about you.

Let's talk about the art of showing up. It begins with posture—eyes forward, shoulders relaxed, chin level, a breath that doesn't sound like a sigh but a deliberate, steady invitation for others to meet you halfway. It continues with small agreements you make with yourself: one "yes" you say to a social event you would have skipped in the past, one boundary you set with a family member who treats your time as an afterthought, one commitment to journal your needs for the week, not to bend to someone else's agenda. When you practice these micro-choices, you're not fabricating bravery—you're producing evidence of it. You become the person who can be counted on to show up, not the person who will excuse herself into the couch at the first sign of discomfort.

The practical side of this is easier than it sounds. Keep a tiny victory log, a place to jot one concrete display of confidence each day. It could be as simple as "I asked for a seat closer to the air vent in the doctor's office" or "I held eye contact, smiled, and spoke clearly during a group chat." Seeing the pattern over weeks helps you notice that confidence is stitched together from many small threads: punctuality for appointments, boundary-setting in a group chat that's spiraling, or choosing a comfortable outfit and wearing it with the intention of feeling like you deserve to be seen. The more you rehearse these moments, the less you rely on a sudden surge of mood to carry you through. And when fear still taps you on the shoulder—the way a neighbor's dog barks at four in the afternoon—you respond with a practiced phrase you've stored away in your memory bank: I've got this, and I'll handle it in my own time.

Confidence is not about pretending you have all the answers or never feeling a twinge of doubt. It's about knowing the right questions to ask, choosing the right actions to take, and accepting that your value doesn't disappear when your voice shakes for a moment. You have earned the right to be visible, to have your needs heard, and to be heard with warmth and humor intact. This is not a performance; it's your life—built deliberately, step by step, with plenty of laughter in the wings and the occasional well-timed wink to the audience of your doubters.

As you move forward, let the confidence you practice become a quiet, reliable partner that doesn't demand perfection but does demand you show up. Tomorrow's small choice could be the one that reminds you of the power you carry simply by being you—no apologies, no caveats, just a steady, brave, very human presence that says, I'm here, and I'm still the star of my own story.

STYLE THAT SERVES YOU (NOT THE INTERNET)

Here's a truth you already know in your bones: fashion trends come and go with the speed of a sneeze. In your sixties, the internet's endless scroll can make you feel as if your wardrobe needs a full reboot every season, even when you're still folding laundry in the same soft cardigan you've loved for years. But style isn't about chasing the newest silhouette or the most photographed outfit; it's about creating a look that honors your today—your curves, your energy cycles, your mobility, and your mood. Style is personal autonomy wearing well-cut fabric, with the goal of ease and expression rather than a mirror's approval. Let's treat your closet as a toolbox and your outfits as practical choices that help you move through the day with dignity, humor, and a dash of sparkle.

Start with comfort that does more than accommodate your body—it invites your life to happen. Fabrics with a little stretch, soft cottons, breathable knits, and breathable moisture-wicking blends can carry you through a morning of errands to an evening of socializing without a wardrobe meltdown. Shoes deserve the same respect: supportive, non-slip soles that still kiss the ground with a little style. Think loafers with a flexible sole, Mary Janes with cushioning, sneakers in a versatile color that goes with everything. If heels make your knees sigh, give them a respectful pass. Your feet know you're aging with grace; your shoes should match that grace, not demand a survival story every time you stand up.

The internet's holy trinity—size, trend, photograph—doesn't have a say in how you feel in your clothes. Your body changes, and that's not a problem to solve but a reality to work with. A tailored silhouette can be your best ally: a blazer in a forgiving stretch fabric can lift your mood and your posture without pinching; a pair of well-cut trousers with a gentle taper can smooth lines and give you a sense of control. Colors are your allies, not your captors. A familiar palette—neutrals you wear confidently, punctuated by a few favorite colors you know make your eyes pop—creates a capsule that travels well, packable and reliable in the chaos of travel plans, grandkid sports events, or coffee dates that turn into unexpected long talks.

Clarity about what you want to communicate through clothing is what saves you from wardrobe anxiety. You want outfits that speak your language: comfort, competence, and a dash of fun. If you're tired by noon, consider a daily uniform—an outfit you can rely on that still feels personal, whether it's a blazer with a soft tee and jeans, or a knit dress with a cardigan you adore. If you crave texture, reach for a knit with a tactile surface, a scarf that can be a last-minute shawl, or a belt that defines your waist without squeezing your breath. Accessorize in ways that feel real to you: a pair of earrings you can sleep in, a watch you can rely on, a scarf that doubles as a shawl on chilly mornings.

Style that serves you also means knowing when to season your life with play. A bright piece, a print you love, a surprising color in a small dose—these are not vanity; they're anchors for joy. You deserve clothes that invite you to participate in the world rather than fade into the background. Your fashion choices can be both functional and expressive, a daily ritual of self-respect and humor. Treat your wardrobe as a conversation with yourself: what do you need today to feel like yourself, and what small adjustment could make that feeling easier to wear? The rest of your life may feel heavier at times, but your style doesn't have to. It can stay light, flexible, and true.

If there's a single practical shift to start with, it's this: audit with honesty, not shame. Remove what hurts or restricts you, keep what you love and actually wear, and tailor what you keep so it fits your current body. A hem that is a touch shorter, a sleeve that sits just so, a waistband that doesn't dig—the details that make a day feel less like a tiny negotiation and more like a moment you can own with ease. When you step into clothes that fit, that move with you, you step into a mindset that values your present, not a past idea of how you should look. And that, in turn, frees you to focus your energy on what you want to do, who you want to be with, and how you want to be seen in the world.

Ultimately, style at sixty-something isn't about pleasing strangers or pursuing internet accolades. It's about choosing outfits that support your activities, honor your comfort, and reflect your inner light. It's about showing up in a way that feels true to your own sense of humor, your own pace, and your own idiosyncrasies. The goal is simple: to walk through your day with posture, poise, and pleasure, rather than fatigue and frustration. When you land on that balance, you'll discover your personal style isn't lost; it's refined, sharpened, and ready to star in the next chapter of your life.

In the weeks ahead, you might notice the days when your clothes feel like a friend rather than a debate. That's the signal you're onto something real: your style is serving you, not the endless tide of online fashion, and that makes every morning something to look forward to rather than dread.

MOVING YOUR BODY WITHOUT PUNISHMENT

Imagine a world where movement isn't a form of punishment for what you ate last night or a reminder that you're not as spry as you once were. Imagine instead a daily ritual where your joints, muscles, and breath work in harmony, where every stretch is a tiny act of kindness toward the body that has carried you through decades of stories. This is the heart of moving your body without punishment. It's about mobility, mood, and freedom—the sense that you can reach, bend, walk, stand, sit, and move with ease, even when creaky doors and creaking knees try to steal the show. Movement becomes a practical ally rather than a moral verdict.

Your body is not a problem to solve; it's a system evolving in response to your life. The goal is not to erase the years but to maximize the joy you can squeeze from a single day. Start with a reframe: the purpose of movement is to preserve options. When you build flexibility in your joints and strengthen the muscles that support your posture, you don't just feel physically better; you also cultivate a more buoyant mood. A ten-minute morning routine can set the tone for the entire day. It might begin with a gentle march in place, calves and ankles waking up after long nights of rest. From there, a few controlled stretches —neck, shoulders, hips, hamstrings—done slowly and with mindful breathing. The kind of breath you use matters as much as the movement itself; a steady inhale through the nose, a slow exhale through the mouth can calm the nervous system and reduce the irritability of sudden stiffness.

The secret to longevity in movement is consistency, not intensity. When you treat movement as a nonnegotiable, you create a rhythm that your body can anticipate. You don't need to join a gym to get traction; a flight of stairs, a park bench, and a set of light-resistant bands in a drawer can be enough to coax real change over weeks. Mobility sits at the intersection of strength and flexibility. It's a dance between muscle engagement and joint range—a careful choreography that expands your options. If a joint feels tight, don't push through the pain or pretend it doesn't exist. Instead, honor its signal by modifying the exercise, shortening the range, or substituting a gentler movement that achieves the same intention—to keep you moving without alarming your nervous system.

A practical approach is to assign movement to your daily anchors. Do a short routine after breakfast, another after lunch, and a longer session if energy and time permit. It's not about conquering a big goal but about maintaining curiosity: can you reach for a high shelf without needing a stool today? Can you walk the length of the grocery store without your breath catching? Can you stand at a sink long enough to wash your hair without tensing up your back? These are the daily tests that accumulate into confidence; they're the quiet evidence that you still own your body, even when it's changed its mind about what it can do.

If you're ever tempted to conflate movement with failure, remember this mantra: progress is personal and incremental. Some days you'll move with a spring in your step; other days you'll move with patience and grace. On all days, you'll choose something that keeps you within your comfort zone while gently expanding your boundaries. That is the essence of moving without punishment. It's the art of treating your body as a partner, not a project—and you'll find that when you nurture that relationship, your mood follows, your energy returns, and your days suddenly hold more hours of possibility than you expected.

As you continue, let the next section be a tool for clear, honest communication about your needs. Saying what you mean is not about being sharp or punitive; it's about ensuring you're heard and understood, so you can move with ease and be treated with respect.

THE POWER OF SAYING WHAT YOU MEAN

Clear words are a superpower you already own but may have learned to hide under a bushel of politeness and fear of conflict. The truth is simple: when you say what you mean in a way that respects both yourself and others, you cut through the noise and create space for real connection. You don't have to be loud to be seen; you have to be honest enough to deliver your message with precision, warmth, and a touch of humor. In the years you've lived, you've learned how to navigate the minefields of family gatherings, medical appointments, and long-held assumptions about what you should want or need. This is your chance to refine that voice into a practical tool for thriving in retirement and beyond.

Saying what you mean starts with a framework that can feel awkward at first but becomes natural with a little practice. Lead with I statements that reflect your own experience and needs rather than accusations about others. It's a small shift, but it changes the dynamic from defensiveness to collaboration. I feel overwhelmed when meetings run late and I haven't been able to digest the information you've sent; I would appreciate a summary email afterward so I can review at my own pace. I'm not comfortable with that tone in our group chat; I'd prefer we keep things constructive and kind, and I'll contribute accordingly. It's not about perfection, but about ensuring your voice matters in the most practical way possible.

Boundaries are the scaffolding that support this voice. They aren't punitive fences; they're the rails that keep your time and energy from derailing in conversations that go off track. You have a lifetime of examples for why your boundaries are reasonable and necessary, and you can deploy them with grace. For instance, when a family member asks you to take on a task that will exhaust you, respond with a calm, specific limit: I can help with this project but not this week; let's set a time for the following week. When a colleague pushes for approval on a project you don't feel ready to sign off on, you can say, I need more information and a plan that addresses these concerns before I commit. These phrases are not confrontational weapons; they're invitations to a clearer, more productive working relationship.

The practical magic lies in the gentle art of repetition. You practice the same phrases in everyday situations—ordering coffee, selecting a restaurant, replying to a friend's invitation that you know comes with a heavy schedule. With time, your speech becomes a map you can navigate with confidence instead of a high-wire act you fear falling off. You begin to notice how the room responds to you when your words are precise and kind. You notice how meetings flow more smoothly when you're clear about your limits. You notice how your own shoulders relax when you've stated your needs instead of swallowing them whole. The result is not a victory of aggression but a win for dignity: you're heard, you're respected, and you still maintain the warmth and humor that are your hallmarks.

So practice daily, not perfection. Read the room not to prove you're tough, but to ensure you're part of the conversation. And if a moment of friction arises, lean into your core confidence—the sense that you've earned your voice through years of listening, learning, and choosing to speak up when it matters most. By the time you apply this to your most delicate conversations, you'll find that the hardest part isn't saying what you mean; it's letting go of the old habit of filtering yourself to fit someone else's idea of how you should be. Your truth is not a risk; it's a bridge to better, more honest connections.

And the last practice you'll want to carry forward is identifying your personal joy list—your reason for choosing a life that reflects who you are—so you can speak from that place with unwavering clarity and a smile.

YOUR PERSONAL JOY LIST

Joy is not a luxury reserved for rare weekends with perfect weather. Joy is a practical resource, a little fuel tank you can refill when the days feel crowded or when you've forgotten what your own laughter sounds like. Your personal joy list is a curated set of activities, loves, and rituals that light you up from the inside out, and it's not a vanity project. It's a strategic, honest inventory of what makes your heart quicker, your step lighter, and your mood more expansive. It can be as simple as a warm mug on a balcony at sunrise, a quick call with a friend who knows your stories, or as bold as a Sunday morning kayak trip or a 15-minute dance session in your living room. The goal is not to measure happiness against youth's standard but to build a resilient supply of moments that remind you just how good it can feel to be you in your own skin.

Begin with a candid inventory. What activities have you enjoyed in the last year that you can fit into your weekly rhythm? Which moments have you lost because you let the day get crowded with obligations or because you talked yourself out of trying something new? Do not censor the list for fear of being silly or too energetic; write it all down, from the big to the small, the adventurous to the comforting. Then give each item a practical home in your calendar. A weekly stroll with a friend might be scheduled like a vital appointment; a monthly pottery class could be penciled in as a treat; a daily five-minute stretch paired with a favorite song becomes a nonnegotiable routine. The point is that joy should be planned as purposefully as meals or doctor appointments, not left to chance.

Next, learn to guard your joy against the intrusions of a busy life. Boundaries don't just apply to the hard conversations; they apply to your time and attention as well. If a family project threatens to swallow your entire weekend, you have a right to propose a compromise that preserves at least a portion of your joy. If a social invitation would drain your energy, you're allowed to decline with grace and still maintain the relationship. Your joy list is not a trophy shelf; it's a living system designed to keep your days from shrinking into a blur of obligations. It should feel like a map that glows softly in the night, guiding you toward moments that remind you why you chose this life in the first place.

Inevitably, the joy list will evolve as you do. Some items will disappear, others will appear, and that's not a failure but a healthy sign of growth. You may discover that you once loved late-night gatherings but now crave quieter evenings with a book and a cup of tea. You may find that you want to explore new hobbies or return to ones you'd set aside. The beauty of this process is in its flexibility and its repeatability. Each week, you can adjust the list, add a new item that excites you, and remove something that no longer fits. It is your personal treasure map—one that points to the moments you want to collect and the stories you want to tell later.

As you incorporate the joy list into daily life, you'll notice that your confidence deepens, not from chasing the impossible but from actively choosing the experiences that resonate with who you are now. You'll discover that you can say yes to joy without feeling you're neglecting responsibility, and you'll begin to understand that joy is not a reward for maturity; it is a practice that sustains it. The more you lean into what truly lights you up, the more your life feels like a stage where you decide the script, walk the line, and deliver your lines with the timing and humor that only you bring to the scene. The next time someone asks what you want to do, you'll have a ready excuse—an authentic list of joys that you're excited to live out, one moment at a time.

THE SWEET FREEDOM OF THIS SEASON —KEEP LAUGHING, KEEP CHOOSING YOU

WHAT YOU KNOW NOW THAT YOU DIDN'T AT 40

If your younger self could drop in for a surprise visit, she'd arrive with a glittery cape and a stubborn question: what happened to the years? And you'd laugh, because you know the answer already, even if she doesn't want to hear it. You've lived long enough to collect a few hard-won truths that your 40-year-old self would have folded into a letter to be opened at every major life milestone: a good day is built on quiet boundaries, not heroic chaos; energy is a renewable resource, so you treat it like a tiny sacred thing; and humor isn't a luxury but a survival mechanism that ages as gracefully as you intend to age. You know, with a certain relief, that the plot isn't collapsing, it's expanding—and you're not the sidekick. You're the author, with a better sense of what actually matters.

You've learned to guard your time the way you guard a favorite cardigan: with care, with selective fabric, and with the knowledge that a single snag can ruin the whole day if you let it. You've discovered that saying no is not a condemnation of your generosity but a rescue of your stamina. Boundaries aren't about putting people in their place; they're about gifting yourself back to yourself—with room to breathe, to dream, to eat what you want without apology, to move in a way that doesn't require a special occasion. It's a kind of quiet revolution, done with warmth and a wink.

There's wisdom in the little losses, too. The glasses that vanish mid-sentence turn into a daily reminder to rebuild rituals—where you put the emergency pair, where you stack the backups, how you label a box of "someday I'll need this" items so they don't become a scavenger hunt when you're late for a doctor appointment. You've learned that forgetfulness isn't a failing; it's a prompt to simplify, to create systems that serve you rather than betray you. It's easier to walk into a room and remember what you were seeking when you've built a tiny, forgiving map of your day. And when you misplace your phone but find the moment you needed it most, you realize you've gained a knack for prioritizing presence over panic.

The body, too, has joined the conversation with no-nonsense honesty. It chimes in with new sound effects, and you reply with compassion and a plan. You respect the tempo of your days, the power of regular movement, the stubborn joy of a good night's sleep, and the simple pleasure of moving through the world with less hurry and more intention. You've learned to celebrate small wins—like choosing a healthier snack without turning it into a moral indictment, or taking a walk with a neighbor who makes you laugh so hard your shoulders loosen.

This knowledge matters because it changes how you show up. It gives you permission to keep the promises you make to yourself—the ones you whispered to your future self at 3 a.m. when the world felt noisy and unkind. It means you can say yes to the right adventures and no to the ones that drain you, with a smile and a boundary rope within reach. And because you've earned it, you don't apologize for wanting a lighter, brighter, more honest life. You deserve to live at the pace that fits you, not the pace someone else thinks is appropriate.

So what you know now isn't just trivia from the school of hard knocks. It's your new operating system. It's the firmware that lets you update your expectations without rebooting your entire identity. It's the reminder that aging isn't a curtain call but a backstage pass to the best version of you that's still learning, still laughing, and still choosing you.

As we close this reflection and slide toward what comes next, carry this forward: your wisdom is a compass, your humor is fuel, and your boundaries are your radar. The next section will pull these threads together in a practical, portable way—your Survival Kit Recap—so you can walk outside tomorrow knowing exactly where your power lives and how to deploy it with grace and a grin.

YOUR SURVIVAL KIT RECAP

The survival kit isn't a museum piece you dust off for special occasions. It's your everyday toolkit, tucked into the pocket of your routine, ready to be pulled out the moment life hands you a curveball with a side of chaos. This is where the glitter meets the grit, where practical tools get dressed up in warm, human language, and where the everyday becomes a little brighter because you choose to act, not panic. You've already built the core elements: checklists that keep you from leaving essential items behind and, more importantly, from leaving yourself behind; scripts that help you speak your truth without losing your sense of humor; and mindset shifts that transform aging from a liability into a repertoire of skills and possibilities.

Let's talk about the core pieces in a way you can actually use them. The checklists aren't tries-at-life lists; they're gentle scaffolds. They remind you to reserve time for yourself and to protect your energy as if it were a cherished, fragile plant that will wilt without water of attention. They show up in your day as tiny prompts—Did I drink water today?

Did I move my body in a way that felt good? Did I tell someone what they mean to me? These prompts don't demand perfection; they invite consistency, which is a whole lot more forgiving and a lot more effective.

The scripts are the social shortcuts you wish you'd had when you were younger, but you've earned them now. They're not cold interrogations; they're warm, firm phrases that keep conversations on track without turning into a battlefield. When a doctor's appointment starts with more big words than your brain can decode, you can lean into a simple script that asks for plain language, a yes/no option, and a clear plan for next steps. In a family miscommunication—when someone implies you're overreacting or underinvolved—you have a script that re-centers you with kindness and boundaries, leaving room for respect while you protect your peace.

The mindset shifts are perhaps the most precious gear you carry. Aging becomes not a reduction but a recalibration: more authority over your calendar, more curiosity about what you can still learn, more pride in who you've become. There's an element of rebellious joy in recognizing your right to change your mind, to pivot, to reinvent, to try on a new hobby or a new role in your family, your circle, or your community. Your survival kit isn't about clinging to a version of yourself that no longer serves you; it's about upgrading to the version that knows how to thrive in a world that still needs your sparkle and your boundaries in equal measure.

If you're already inventing your next move while you're reading this, you're using your kit exactly as intended. The tools live in you—your experience, your humor, your stubborn grace—and the kit simply helps you remember to reach for them when needed. You've learned that resilience isn't a cape you wear for emergencies; it's a daily practice, a gentle discipline that keeps you moving in the direction you want to go, even when the road gets rocky or when the group chat turns into a digital soup of opinions.

As the page turns toward the future, keep this handy image in your mind: you, with your Survival Kit, stepping into the next chapter with calm, clarity, and a punchline ready. The future isn't a blank page; it's a canvas already speckled with memories, plans, and possibilities you haven't tried yet. The next section will transport you from the toolkit to a vision you can actually look forward to—a life that expands rather than shrinks, a life that invites you to show up with intention, humor, and full permission to be exactly who you are.

A FUTURE YOU CAN ACTUALLY LOOK FORWARD TO

Imagine a day that begins with the kind of morning you once saved for special occasions—the aroma of coffee, the soft light on the blinds, the plan you crafted the night before, and no urgent emergency demanding your attention before you've even brushed your teeth. This isn't a dream you'll wake from; it's the future you're allowed to claim, one intention at a time. Aging, spoken plainly, is expansion. It's a widening of your circle of influence, a softening of your fears, a sharpening of your humor, and a deepening of your relationship with yourself. The years ahead won't be a quiet descent but a robust ascent into the life you're still capable of building, the people you're still capable of loving, and the activities you still want to explore.

Retirement reinvention isn't about pinning a perpetual vacation to your calendar. It's about designing a life that respects the truth of who you are today and invites the world to meet that version of you with curiosity, not apology. You'll discover you can pursue health and vitality with a gentleness that suits your stamina and a stubborn joy that suits your temperament. The workouts you'll love aren't always the most intense; they're the ones that feel like a celebration of what your body can do, not a punishment for what it cannot endure. A walk through a park becomes a moving meditation, a dance class a chance to reframe your relationship with your body, a swim a quiet victory over the labels aging sometimes tries to place on you.

And there's room for purpose that isn't tethered to a single identity. You can slip into new roles with the ease of someone who has nothing left to prove but has everything to gain: a mentor, a volunteer, a guide to a younger friend, a creator of little rituals that anchor your days. Travel awaits, in bursts of weekend adventures or longer journeys when you're ready. You'll find joy in small, repeatable routines—daily stretches that call your breath back, reading lists that keep your curiosity alive, and conversations that challenge you to stay curious, kind, and bold. It's not about pretending you're still twenty; it's about choosing the energy and the curiosity you still have, and giving yourself permission to enjoy them without apology.

In this future, technology becomes a tool that serves you, not a mystery you fear. You'll plan for the quirks of aging with a sense of humor: devices that sometimes misbehave become comedy partners, nudging you toward patience, problem-solving, and a smile that refuses to fade. Your social world will expand in meaningful ways—new friends who groan with you at the same jokes, grandkids who teach you a new slang word and remind you that love doesn't grow smaller with time. You'll build boundaries that protect your presence in the lives you care about, and you'll give yourself permission to say yes to the things that ignite your passion and no to the things that dim your light.

A future you can look forward to isn't a denial of reality; it's a celebration of progress, a deliberate choice to keep evolving while staying true to the core of who you are. The more you lean into this expansion, the more your days begin to hum with possibility. And as you picture that future, you'll find the courage to begin shaping it today, one small, joyful decision at a time. The next part of our journey invites you to name that courage in one brave action—so you can prove to yourself that you're not just dreaming the moment, you're living it.

As you turn from vision to action, remember that the world doesn't demand perfection from you; it asks only for your engagement, your kindness, and your brave authenticity. The next section will give that gentle shove—the One Brave Thing you can choose to do this week to start shaping the life you're already claiming in your imagination.

THE "ONE BRAVE THING" CHALLENGE

What if the next week could become a turning point by a single, doable act that matters more than a thousand half-hearted intentions? That's the heart of the One Brave Thing Challenge: choose one small action that expands your freedom, honors your boundaries, or invites a fresh kind of joy into your days. The key is to pick something so manageable that you can't talk yourself out of it, and so meaningful that skipping it feels like denying a version of yourself you've decided to honor. You'll do it, you'll own it, and you'll tell someone about it so you don't let it slip away into the busy blur of ordinary life.

Perhaps your brave thing is a boundary set with a difficult family member, a message written to a friend you've been meaning to reconnect with, or a coaching call booked that you've allowed to orbit your calendar like a rumor for months. Maybe it's a small public display of your worth—a bold outfit you adore but have saved for a "special occasion," or a short trip you plan with a friend who makes you feel seen and safe at the same time. It could be something as simple as a five-minute daily ritual that returns you to your breath and your center after a long day, or a phone call to a doctor or service provider you've postponed because you were worried about being a bother. The point is not what the brave thing is, but that you name it, commit to it, and do it.

How do you choose? Look for something

that would make your life more aligned with the version of yourself you're proud to be. It should feel like a punch of momentum rather than a push of guilt. You'll set a date, you'll tell a trusted friend or partner what you're doing, and you'll celebrate the small victory no matter the outcome. If you stumble, you'll reframe the stumble as information, not a failure—learn what blocked you, adjust, and try again. This isn't about proving yourself to the world; it's about proving to yourself that your agency still has backbone, still has humor, and still has room to grow.

In the week ahead, you might choose to text the person you've been avoiding because you fear conflict, or you might schedule a wellness check with your doctor that you've been delaying because you'd rather pretend you're invincible. You could don a bright scarf and walk into a room where you used to shrink, or you could finally press "send" on a dating app message you've drafted four times and never sent. The exact bravery isn't as important as the act of choosing yourself in a small, concrete way.

When you reach the end of the seven days, you'll review not only what you did but how it felt to do it. If the feeling was light and true, you've found your rhythm. If it was heavier than expected, you've learned more about your boundaries and your patience. Either way, you've built momentum that proves you're still worth the courage you've allowed yourself to demand and deserve.

The One Brave Thing is a habit you can repeat—not as a stunt but as a practice of showing up for yourself. And that practice—like any good comedy—gets better with repetition, with a willingness to fail, and with a generous dose of self-kindness that lets you laugh at yourself when you forget the script and still show up anyway.

Now take a breath, pick your brave thing, and set a date. The next section will take your bravery and turn it into a final pep talk that feels like a warm hug and a bright future all in one.

FINAL PEP TALK: YOU'RE NOT FADING—YOU'RE EDITING

Here's the truth you've earned the right to claim: aging isn't a dimming of your light; it's a recalibration of your lighting rig. You're not fading into a background you can't quite hear over the tapping of the clock; you're editing your life with precision, humor, and a fierce sense of self-respect. You get to decide what deserves your spotlight, what deserves your time, and what deserves a gentle, perhaps stubborn, no. And that is freedom—the sweet, stubborn freedom of this season.

You've learned to trim the noise and amplify the notes that matter. You've practiced naming what you want, and you've practiced asking for it with kindness and clarity. You've seen that boundaries aren't fences to trap you but bridges to safer, more honest connections. You've discovered that companionship can be chosen and cultivated at any age, that friendship can be a source of strength rather than a source of drama, and that the right people will meet you where you are without requiring you to apologize for your truth.

Laughter stays your most reliable companion. It is the sound that travels through a crowded room and lands in your chest with a surprising zing, reminding you that you're not done learning, not done laughing, not done loving. The lines on your face tell a map of stories—each one a chapter where you chose resilience over resignation, humor over helplessness, and grace over grievance. You've earned every anecdote and every ache that makes your life feel fully lived, not merely endured. And you've earned the right to feel powerful in your own body, to celebrate your style, and to present your most authentic self to the world without apology.

The plan for the next chapter is simple, even when life gets complicated: protect your time, nurture your energy, and remain curious. Build a daily ritual that honors your needs, not the noise of others' expectations. Keep a small, brave project in motion—a hobby, a class, a volunteer gig—that keeps your mind active and your heart engaged. Surround yourself with people who reflect your best self, who cheer you on, who challenge you with warmth, and who remember that the goal is not perfection but flourishing. And when you stumble, as you will, treat yourself with the same compassion you would offer a dear friend who's learning to fly again.

You are not a fading note in a fading song. You are an entire orchestra, practicing your craft, composing your own finale, and playing it with gusto. You're editing, not erasing; refining, not eroding. The future isn't a question mark; it's a chorus you're building one line at a time—a chorus that includes more laughter, sharper boundaries, deeper connections, and more joy than you've allowed yourself to dream in years.

So go forward with humor as your compass and self-trust as your ballast. Keep choosing you, keep rewriting your scenes, and keep laughing at the glorious mess of it all. This book may be finished, but your journey isn't closed. It's a living, evolving script—and you hold the pen.

www.ingramcontent.com/pod-product-compliance
Lightning Source LLC
Chambersburg PA
CBHW071339080526
44587CB00017B/2893